"Admittedly not a joiner, I most certainly did not see myself being part of the *She's Got Issues* club. Not only did I find myself in the club Unice so aptly describes, but I joyfully found I was not alone there. Nicole Unice knows women, and she knew me in a way I did not yet know myself."

MARGOT STARBUCK
Author of *Unsqueezed: Springing Free from Skinny Jeans, Nose Jobs, Highlights and Stilettos*

"If you're a woman, if you have issues—then it's simple. This book is for you!"

RENEE JOHNSON FISHER
Author of *Faithbook of Jesus* and *Not Another Dating Book*

"Nicole is hip, hilarious, and nakedly vulnerable. Her teaching is meaty and her advice, real-world doable. That's seriously good news for you and me!"

LESA ENGELTHALER
Writer, Redbud Writers Guild; nonprofit executive recruiter, Victory Search Group

"Nicole Unice is the perfect girlfriend to hash out issues like insecurity or anger with. Her authentic style, hard-hitting stories, and poignant biblical truth will encourage you to get real about your stuff and move you from an 'ordinary' life to a fully abundant life."

SARAH FRANCIS MARTIN
Author of *Stress Point: Thriving through Your Twenties in a Decade of Drama*

"Nicole offers a real gift to women who feel stuck in life. This practical, fun-to-read book is packed with life-freeing wisdom. *She's Got Issues* will help women everywhere learn to see their 'issues' in a whole new transformative light."

CARYN DAHLSTRAND RIVADENEIRA
Author of *Grumble Hallelujah*; founding member of Redbud Writers Guild

"I won't pretend. I've got issues—all kinds of them. Likely you do too, so pull up a chair and let Nicole chat hope and help into yours."

ELISA MORGAN
Author of *She Did What She Could*, www.sdwsc.com; publisher of *FullFill*, www.fullfill.org

"*She's Got Issues* sees that unsettled place deep within us and provides a path toward abundance. Read it and rest assured: God is not limited by your issues."

AMY SIMPSON
Editor, *Gifted for Leadership* and *Kyria*'s Marriage & Parenting resources, Christianity Today

"With warmth and wisdom, Nicole exposes the lies that hold us captive. She leads us by the hand to God's grace and mercy, and we are offered fresh hope."

JO SAXTON
Director, 3DM; author of *Real God, Real Life*

"If you're sick of a life of superficial smiles and saccharine, so-so-faith, Nicole Unice invites you into a raw conversation about the real-life issues that hold us back. *She's Got Issues* is refreshing in its honesty, convicting in its insight, and inspiring in its applications."

KELLI B. TRUJILLO
Author of *Faith-Filled Moments* and *The Busy Mom's Guide to Spiritual Survival*

"It takes only a few pages to realize that Nicole is the kind of woman who is comfortable exposing her issues while challenging us to deal with ours. *She's Got Issues* acknowledges 'the ache of the ordinary' from a woman who gets it, who's lived it, and who doesn't want any of us settling for it."

JENNI CATRON
Executive Director, Cross Point Church; founder of Cultivate Her

"The apostle Paul tells us not to grow weary in doing good; yet that weariness is where many of us live. Nicole Unice has lived there too. She writes with transparency and a touch of humor about what can move us toward the authentic, abundant life Jesus promises. *She's Got Issues* offers a brand-new zip code."

MICHELLE VAN LOON
Communications director of Christ Together/Chicago; author of *Uprooted: Growing a Parable Life from the Inside Out*

"I'm so glad Nicole wrote this book! She blends her life experiences with the truth of the Bible to bring our struggles to light and to show us how God can make us into the women he's created us to be."

LAURA DWIGHT
Student, University of South Carolina

"'Hi, my name is Tracey and I'm a control freak with issues.' With her utterly winsome, engaging, and savvy voice, Nicole Unice makes it okay for us to admit it all, to confess our shortcomings, and to find our way to life-giving change."

TRACEY BIANCHI
Pastor for Women's Ministry at Christ Church of Oak Brook, writer, speaker, and activist

"Nicole invites you to recognize those things that have left you frustrated and longing for more. She will guide you with biblical depth to a place of hope and engagement so that God can transform your life for His purposes."

JACKY GATLIFF
National Director, Women In Ministry, Evangelical Presbyterian Church

"I have issues, and I'm so glad my friend Nicole Unice wrote about them. She provides real-life assessment, on-target analysis, and oh-so-practical solutions."

JUDY DOUGLASS
Author, speaker; director of women's resources, Cru

SHE'S GOT ISSUES

*seriously good news for stressed-out,
secretly scared control freaks like us*

NiCOLE UNiCE

TYNDALE
MOMENTUM®

*The nonfiction imprint of
Tyndale House Publishers, Inc.*

Visit Tyndale online at www.tyndale.com.

Visit Tyndale Momentum online at www.tyndalemomentum.com.

Visit the author at www.nicoleunice.com.

TYNDALE, Tyndale Momentum, and Tyndale's quill logo are registered trademarks of Tyndale House Publishers, Inc. The Tyndale Momentum logo is a trademark of Tyndale House Publishers, Inc. Tyndale Momentum is the nonfiction imprint of Tyndale House Publishers, Inc., Carol Stream, Illinois.

She's Got Issues: Seriously Good News for Stressed-Out, Secretly Scared Control Freaks Like Us

Copyright © 2012 by Nicole Unice. All rights reserved.

Cover photograph copyright © Joellen L. Armstrong/Shutterstock. All rights reserved.

Author photograph copyright © 2011 by Kate Magee Photography. All rights reserved.

Designed by Jacqueline L. Nuñez

Published in association with MacGregor Literary Agency, 2373 NW 185th Ave, Suite 165, Hillsboro, OR 97124.

Unless otherwise indicated, all Scripture quotations are taken from the *Holy Bible*, New Living Translation, copyright © 1996, 2004, 2007 by Tyndale House Foundation. (Some quotations may be from the NLT1, copyright © 1996.) Used by permission of Tyndale House Publishers, Inc., Carol Stream, Illinois 60188. All rights reserved.

Scripture quotations marked NIV are taken from the Holy Bible, *New International Version,*® NIV.® Copyright © 1973, 1978, 1984, 2011 by Biblica, Inc.® (Some quotations may be from the earlier NIV edition, copyright © 1984.) Used by permission. All rights reserved worldwide.

Scripture quotations marked NKJV are taken from the New King James Version,® copyright © 1982 by Thomas Nelson, Inc. Used by permission. All rights reserved.

Scripture quotations marked *The Message* are taken from *THE MESSAGE*, copyright © 1993, 1994, 1995, 1996, 2000, 2001, 2002, by Eugene H. Peterson. Used by permission of NavPress. All rights reserved. Represented by Tyndale House Publishers, Inc.

Scripture quotations marked NASB are taken from the New American Standard Bible,® copyright © 1960, 1962, 1963, 1968, 1971, 1972, 1973, 1975, 1977, 1995 by The Lockman Foundation. Used by permission.

The names and identifying details of many of the women and families whose stories appear in this book have been changed to protect their privacy.

For information about special discounts for bulk purchases, please contact Tyndale House Publishers at csresponse@tyndale.com, or call 1-800-323-9400.

Library of Congress Cataloging-in-Publication Data

Unice, Nicole.
  She's got issues : seriously good news for stressed-out, secretly scared control freaks like us / Nicole Unice.
    p. cm.
  Includes bibliographical references (p.   ).
  ISBN 978-1-4143-6510-7 (sc)
1. Christian women—Religious life.   I. Title.
  BV4527.U55 2012
  248.8'43—dc23   2012000819

Printed in the United States of America

23   22   21   20   19   18
13   12   11   10   9   8

For Olivia:

Talitha koum!

"In this world you will have trouble, but take heart!

I have overcome the world."   *—Jesus*

CONTENTS

ACKNOWLEDGMENTS

I AM IN AWE OF THIS JOB OF CRAFTING WORDS. Not just any words, but words that I pray would breathe life into your heart. Because these words are about the Word himself, the ultimate healer of hearts and liberator of souls. So my first gratitude goes to Jesus for his love for me. All the words in the world could not express my thanks. I am indebted to him and surrendered to everything he asks.

I would not be a woman of substance without the unconditional love of my husband. Dave, since the moment you told me you loved me, you've continued to love me faithfully and with a heart of gold. I don't know how you do it, and I marvel at the mystery and richness of this love. Thanks for always believing in me, especially when I didn't believe in myself.

To my children, Charlie, Cameron, Desmond, who think I can do anything—you love me in my strength, but more important, you love me in my weakness. I am so grateful for God's grace to sustain you in the places where I fail. I can only hope to teach you as much about love, joy, and mercy as you've taught me.

To my parents, Steve and Carleene; my sister, Jen; and my brother, Matt; and to Laura, Tracy, Paul, and Lynne: you have showed me extravagant grace as I've turned into a hermit to write this book. Thanks for the many ways you loved our family in my absence.

Jacky Gatliff, Keri Wyatt Kent, Caryn Rivadeniera, Laura Polk, Tracey Bianchi: you saw a spark in me and fanned it into flame. God is good to intersect our paths. Thanks also to Carolyn Custis James and the Synergy Network for making that connection even easier.

Pete Bowell and David Dwight, pastors of Hope Church: your character and fidelity speak even louder than your leadership and wisdom. If I referenced you for every spiritual insight I've gleaned and written here, you'd have to be my coauthors . . . but I wasn't sure you wanted your debut book to be about women's issues.

To Becca P. and Stacie M.: you read my words and edited with a light hand and an encouraging heart. I hope I can return the favor in this lifetime.

Carrie, Melissa, Lisa, Christy, Sarah, Sarah, Jen: You are friends for life. We can cry, laugh, encourage, comfort, and confront (and tease), all in one conversation. My cup overflows.

Jes, Cody, Kristy, Ryan, Drew, and Patrick: you've come into my life and brought joy to my heart. The way you love my kids and love God is astounding to me. I cannot wait to see the next chapters of your lives unfold. Thanks for letting me be your life coach, surrogate mom, and friend. I consider it a great honor.

Sandra, the wonder agent: I sort of landed on your doorstep and you took me in anyway. You were faithful to believe in me, to pray for me, to promote me. When I think of you, I smile. I could never have done this without a friend for an agent, and I consider you a friend. Thank you, and here's to many more projects together.

Jan: our two-hour coffee was a defining moment last year. The love and interest you showed for my life with Jesus, my life in counseling, and my life as a writer—I'm living the dream. Thanks for taking a chance on me! And to the rest of the marketing and editing team at Tyndale: I feel like I've come home. You've cared for my message and made it even better. I'm honored.

INTRODUCTION

I'm a hazard to myself.

PINK

IS BEING A CHRISTIAN SUPPOSED TO CHANGE ME?

Not the kind of change that happens to coffee when you stir in sugar. The kind of change I expected out of Christianity wouldn't take something sweet and lay it over something bitter so that it seemed different but remained the same underneath. The kind of change I was expecting would be about something entirely different. After all, the Bible tells us that if we follow Jesus, we are "new": new birth, new creation, new nature, new person. But until I began to ask that question—really ask it—I think I was just the same old me, with a sugar packet or two of Christianity sprinkled on top.

The question of change came in the midst of an avalanche of ordinary. In our attempt to live the American dream, my family—husband, two toddlers, and dog—moved to a new home in a better school district approximately sixty seconds before I was due to give birth to my third child. At least it felt like a scant minute: the frantic packing and unpacking, taking down pictures, putting up cribs. The toddlers watched endless television, and I had an endless ache in my back.

And when the baby finally came, it was then—with a new

child, a new home, a new neighborhood, and the still-real feeling of being a relatively new mom—that I began to question just what following Christ was all about.

The mental haze and physical exhaustion that come with young children had stripped away my normal nice-girl demeanor, and the results weren't pretty. I wrestled with my out-of-control heart by taking it out on my husband, giving orders about the proper way to load the dishwasher, to bathe a child, to hold a pacifier, even the proper way to hug me ("Not a side hug, honey; I need a *real* hug! Hug me like you mean it!"). I was constantly comparing myself—my career, my waistline, the organizational status of my closets—to other women, desperately seeking some place to find satisfaction. I was buried under the ordinary.

It was a day like the day before and the one before that, when the late afternoon hours seem to last a year. The baby whined, slung across my forearm. I drummed out a monotonous rhythm with the baby-laden arm while my free hand stirred together pasta and rotisserie chicken, something I would try to pass off as dinner. When my husband walked through the door that evening, I stopped stirring the who-cares dinner and passed the baby to his waiting hands in a glorious handoff worthy of the Super Bowl.

I stepped out onto the front porch to throw my head back and roll my shoulders and try—again—to get my filter back in place, to get back to nice-girl-nice-mom-all-together status. With tears of frustration threatening to erupt like a thunderstorm, I looked down my pretty street: a predictable cul-de-sac, green lawns, blue skies, and pink crepe myrtles. My swirling thoughts defied my weariness, when that question raced in and parked itself in the front of my mind: *Is being a Christian supposed to change me?*

Some of my neighbors are Christians, some aren't. But they are all reasonably nice people living nice lives, raising nice kids—doing their best, just like me. Having bad days, just like me. Just like me . . .

In that sunny moment on my porch, the disparity between what I *said* I believed about the Christian life and what I was *living* became clear to me. It was as if God sliced a cross section of my spirit and laid it under a microscope. Every issue I struggled with on that afternoon—the internal twisting of my own heart, the self-focused wrestling that kept me bound and loveless—came into focus. There was no dramatic issue lurking. I wasn't hiding a secret life or a stormy past. I knew my issues—my ordinary, run-of-the-mill, American-woman issues—wouldn't kill me or land me on *Dr. Phil*. Yet the moment was so sharp and so real, it pierced me through.

Standing on my porch with a dish towel on one shoulder and a burp cloth on the other, I knew in the deepest part of my soul that this could not be the "life to the full" that Jesus promised.

If I didn't have God to transform me in the ordinary stuff of life, if the concept of being made new didn't apply right there on my front porch, right in my ordinary issues, then what is being a Christian about anyway? Being nicer? Because if Jesus is who he says he is, then my existence as a pretty-nice Christian living like everyone else seemed like a mockery of faith.

If you are tired of "life to the full" looking like the same old you with some sugar on top, then you are in good company. If you've ever wondered whether life lived with God can really change you, if you've wondered whether God's offer of freedom and beauty apply right in the middle of your ordinary issues, if you've yearned for a better life, then welcome. May this be the beginning of a new journey for you, one full of wonder at a God who still works miracles, even in the ordinary of our lives.

CHAPTER 1
CHEAP PLASTIC SOULS

I'm a Barbie girl, in a Barbie world.
AQUA

THE MOMENT OF TRUTH on the front porch passed, and I stepped back to life, back to whining babies and tired toddlers and mediocre dinners and brain-dead evenings on the couch. But the door had been flung open, and there was no slamming it shut. And so I did what I do best—I argued with myself about the question that wouldn't leave me alone: *Am I changed because of Jesus?*

First I told myself why I was qualified to decide if I was changed: I'm a counselor, for heaven's sake. I'm a supposed expert on how to be a healthy person.

Then I told myself why I was qualified to be a Christian: I rock at Bible trivia games. I am so legit. I can even pronounce a few Hebrew words, and I know the four different Greek words for love. I've gone to seminary!

Then I told myself the truth: I can't really handle ordinary life with a constant peace or lasting joy. I do okay loving when it's easy. I don't love much when it's hard.

I was tired. Tired of pretending that everything was fine, that I had this whole good-Christian thing figured out. Tired of worshiping on Sunday morning and yelling on Sunday afternoon. Tired of knowing the answers but continuing to deal with the same ol' ordinary problems that have been around since middle school.

Maybe it was the scandal of the ordinary that kept me there, thinking mundane, everyday problems were too small for God. Maybe I had bought into the lie that I have the power to deal with any shortcomings myself—other women I knew struggled with the same things and *seemed* perfectly fine.

Chalk my unease up to postpartum hormones or new house adjustments or fatigue. Perhaps if you and I were sitting together, sharing the frustrations of our lives, we would attribute it to circumstances like these. Maybe I'd tell you it would get better in a few weeks. Maybe you'd tell me I just needed a nap. We'd laugh, maybe. We'd call it ordinary. We'd tell each other we'd be okay.

The scandal of the ordinary kept me thinking mundane, everyday problems were too small for God.

Control issues, comparisons, insecurity—commonplace issues of the soul that I finally faced on my front porch—lead to a form of bondage. But because the chains of these issues are so thin, because we don't talk about them much or take them very seriously, we hardly notice their combined effect. We are unaware that these issues hinder us from walking free in the path God has laid out for us. The stuff that affects your inner and outer world might be ordinary, but it's certainly not innocuous.

Take my friend Rachel. I met Rachel when she was a bobble-headed sixth grader, full of chatter and bad jokes, when her most pressing concern was whether to invite one of the girls from Bible study to her sleepover. Friendships and sick uncles and bad quiz grades were her issues. I watched Rachel grow from a frivolous middle schooler into a brooding teenager, wrestling with boundaries and absolutes and the truth about who she really was. And ten years later, Rachel is still wrestling. She's twenty-five and beautiful now. She doesn't ask me to pray about her sleepovers or sick pets anymore, but some of the same issues that first wrapped chains around her in middle school—the ones we call commonplace—are still at work in Rachel's soul. Rachel's getting tired of the insecurity that plagues her, the always-present voice that tells her she's not pretty enough, smart enough, or loving enough to obtain the life she craves. She recognizes the voice and would love to silence it. But she's not sure how.

You may admit that there are some things in your life that hold you back, but you won't hear much about them anywhere else. Ordinary isn't sexy. Ordinary doesn't make headlines. It's not the stuff of e-mail forwards or YouTube videos. Ordinary transformation doesn't send us up to the front of the church to give testimony. "I used to struggle with comparisons, especially when it came to the size of my jeans . . . but now in the power of Jesus' name, I'm free!" I want to be free of comparison, but it's not exactly a moving testimony.

Sometimes I wish I had a story more like my friend Jen's. She lived life to a whole different kind of "full" in college. She ran fast and wild. Our senior year, my friend group called her "the vampire" because she would slide into our dorm from a night-to-morning party when we were slinging on our backpacks and leaving for morning classes. But she lived her wild life with panache, embracing her party-girl reputation while simultaneously earning a double major. When she, out of nowhere, embraced Christianity, I wanted to hold a pep rally for Jesus. Jen's in full-time ministry now. Her dramatic story is real. She became my hope that Christianity actually did work; that Jesus was real; and that people could change. I clung to her story because it helped me believe in a bigger God—probably because when I, the "good" one, talked about my relationship with Jesus, I was about as convincing as a hostess on an infomercial.

So as much as I love the dramatic story of my college friend, what matters in our lives, in the way we love, is the story we are all living right now. My story, Rachel's story, your story—not the YouTube viral video or the e-mail forward or that great testimony in church—is the place where Jesus wants us to demonstrate what "life to the full" means. And our story is deeply affected by everyday issues because they impact every aspect of our lives—our understanding of God, our own emotional and spiritual health, and most certainly our relationships.

SO WHAT'S THIS "ORDINARY"?

We all have roller-coaster-mood days, lapses in judgment that lead to bad decisions, and moments (or months!) of self-centeredness. My front-porch moment was all of that, but more, the culmination of consistent and well-worn patterns popping up like a jack-in-the-box in my life. On further inspection, perhaps what I considered "ordinary" was closer to crazy.

When God laid my heart out in full relief, I was shocked enough that I not only wanted to change but realized how desperately I needed to do so. There's a simple exercise that can help you determine the full reality of your own heart condition. Imagine reading a printout of every thought you've had this week. Now picture yourself taking that printout to your best friend, your small group, and (gasp!) your pastor for them to read. Would you be okay with living that transparently? How different would your inside reality be from your outside persona?

Most days, we filter this "ordinary" existence, hoping to leave the dirty stuff on the inside and put forth the cleanest version of ourselves. But on a bad day or in the dark stillness of interrupted slumber, have your thoughts ever wandered to a startling place of general unease? Have you ever thought, *Is this really all there is? Is this as fulfilled as I can be in this life? Will I ever be who I'm truly meant to be?* These moments are the true revealers of our hearts, showing how puny our "abundant life" really is, how dependent our faith and joy are on feelings and circumstances.

I'm guessing this isn't any surprise to you. I think you want more. We all hope the promise of abundant life is attainable in our lives, but we keep stubbing our toes on obstacles and joy-stealing, love-sucking issues that we don't know how to change.

Sound familiar? It certainly does for me. And after years of living like this, it's not surprising that most of us give up on actually changing. We give our issues cute titles. We shrug off our issues as just "our personality." We call our stubbornness or pride just being a "control freak." We call our anxiety our "concerns." We call a bitter place of unforgiveness a "grudge." We call our insecurity—well, insecurity. Being secure in yourself as a woman? The exception, never the rule!

When we believe that life is as good as it's gonna get, we make an expensive trade in our souls. We stuff away the raw and messy and put forth a nicer but cheaper, plastic version of ourselves. Our story is clean and easy—but also fake. We aren't seeing a true image anymore—the image God made and is making of us—we have built our own "acceptable" image. This is what living with ordinary issues does to us. It slowly kills what is beautiful and unique and turns us into half-dead versions of what we were meant to be.

FINDING REAL ABUNDANCE

If your normal Christian experience is about a fleeting peace, some emergency prayers, or relief that you have an insurance policy for heaven, I can't wait to introduce you to so much more. Although Jesus does offer you eternity with him, he is just as concerned with another aspect of living—the part that happens right in the mess of your ordinary life.

But even the people who walked behind Jesus while his sandals kicked up dust, who shared the same loaf of bread and touched his hands, and knew what his voice sounded like when he first woke up—even they were confused about Jesus and what he offered to them. Near the end of his earthly life, Jesus and his disciples shared a special meal—the Passover. Imagine them reclining around the table, talking about the many things they'd seen through the last few years of doing life together. Imagine how their ears perked up when Jesus, the miracle worker, the interpreter of the law, the center of all the action, looked intently at them and said, "A new command I give you."

Don't you think they leaned in even closer to hear what he would say next?

> Love one another. As I have loved you, so you must love one another. By this all men will know that you are my disciples, if you love one another. (John 13:34-35, NIV)

It's not that Jesus was proclaiming something new: he'd been all about love through the last three years of healing and teaching. But . . . well, is that what it's really all about? That the way we love each other is the way we are to be known to the world?

The number one way we are known as Jesus followers is through, and in, our relationships with one another.

Author Brennan Manning says, "Contact with Christians should be an experience that proves to people that the gospel is a power that transforms the whole of life."[1] Being a disciple when Jesus walked the earth meant following a radical call—not of rebellion but of crazy love that defied earthly expectation. And that hasn't changed. Being a Christian isn't just about going to heaven. It's about a power that transforms your whole life. Your thoughts. Your behaviors. Your relationships. Your love.

SO . . . HOW'S LOVE GOING FOR YOU?

If the grocery store cashier or your kid's teacher or the last waiter who served you described you with complete honesty, would *loving* be the first word he or she would use? Or would you be known by some other nicety, like *control freak* or *frazzled* or *scared*?

Here's the *craziest part* of our ordinary issues: we often have no idea how these issues kill our ability to love powerfully and unconditionally. We all intend to be loving. We try to do a good job of it, but when we are living with a half-dead heart or a plastic existence, we aren't capable of loving the way we'd like. A withered heart just doesn't respond the way we want. And no power of will or self-talk or knowledge can change that.

I have a twentysomething friend who struggles with comparison. She intends to love well. She wants to be happy with her friends when they have a date or a job interview, but the issue of comparison has a hold on her heart. She is so busy evaluating what she doesn't have that she has no energy to be happy for what her girlfriends do have. Her intense preoccupation with self is just one example of how our ordinary issues cripple our ability to love—even our own friends!

Peter, a disciple of Jesus who had control and comparison issues in his early life, later admonished believers to "be self-controlled and alert. Your enemy the devil prowls around like a roaring lion looking for someone to devour" (1 Peter 5:8, NIV). As my friend discovered, even ordinary issues can create destruction in your life.

DO YOU HAVE ISSUES?

The ability to see yourself clearly is crucial in your relationship with Christ and in your subsequent ability to serve well. You cannot live more abundantly and love better without addressing the underlying issues. You are not after perfection in the way you love, but you do need to cultivate a growing dependency on a relationship with Christ that gives you the ability to love.

The first step, then, is assessing your heart condition. To do that, you need to look for the three signs of an issue-laden life. Think of the way fatigue relates to anemia, or sniffles to the cold, or fever to the flu. These symptoms are your first indicator that you've got something going on beneath the surface. Similarly, there are three overarching symptoms in your life that let you know you've got issues: blindness, lack of compassion, and convoluted conflict.

Symptom #1: Blindness

Let me explain how motherhood and triple bathroom mirrors opened my eyes to this condition in myself. When our oldest son started kindergarten, our family moved to a new level of crazy. A young man of rules, Charlie deals with a little fear issue, and every morning he was terrified of the dreaded possibility of *missing the bus*. That could be manageable, except for the three- and one-year-olds who ruled the house like little dictators.

One morning after we had narrowly escaped the dreadful *missing the bus*, I began helping my daughter prepare for preschool. Finally I stole away for sixty seconds of luxurious "me" time: just enough to hurriedly brush my teeth in peace. But as all mothers know, the click of the bathroom lock is the signal for a code-red emergency to break out. On this morning, it was my daughter's unsuccessful search for a pair of matching socks.

"Mama, I need socks!"

"Mommy, I can't find my purple and white socks. Mommy!"

"MOMMY, I need help! MOMMY, where are you? MOMMY!"

"MOMMMMMMYYYY!!!"

I spit into the sink and screamed so loud that my voice scratched as if it were coming from a blown speaker. "BEEEEEeeeeeeee PAaaaaaaTIENT!!!!"

At that moment, I caught a panoramic view of myself in the triple bathroom mirrors. With toothpaste on my lip, hair scrambled on top of my head, and a wild look in my eye, I screamed "Be patient!" like a woman possessed. The mirrors captured the irony of my statement in triplicate. I began to wonder how my own issues were becoming my kids' issues. Ouch.

Eye-opening experiences happen throughout Scripture. Jesus proclaimed that he came to bring "sight to the blind" (Luke 4:18, NKJV). He frequently preached about spiritual and relational blindness, particularly when talking to the so-called spiritual people, the Pharisees:

> You blind guides! You strain out a gnat but swallow a
> camel. "Woe to you, teachers of the law and Pharisees,
> you hypocrites! You clean the outside of the cup
> and dish, but inside they are full of greed and self-
> indulgence. Blind Pharisee! First clean the inside of the
> cup and dish, and then the outside also will be clean."
> (Matthew 23:24-26, NIV)

Heavy words! Even—and especially—the religious leaders seemed prone to a malignant form of blindness. They could preach the Word. They knew the law, and they knew what to do to appear right and good. But Jesus knew the truth about their hearts. The religious show they liked to put on wasn't fooling him.

Our ordinary issues may seem so commonplace that we stay blind to the truth of our own condition. But it's in stories just like mine that we have a choice. We can shrug off reality and use circumstances, personality, or PMS to justify our behavior, or we can face the truth of just how damaging ordinary issues are in our lives. Without that truth, as painful as it might be, we aren't able to access the kind of compassion and love that should characterize our lives. We will be *known* by our love (see John 13:35). That morning in the bathroom mirror gave me eyes to see the reality of my heart: something crazy was lurking beneath the surface. (I also looked crazy, but that's another story.)

Symptom #2: Lack of compassion

This symptom may be the most obvious: the half-dead heart has no compassion reserve. The word *compassion* means "to suffer with," and when we are "suffering with" a bunch of our own stuff, it is almost impossible to offer ourselves freely to someone else. We all find it difficult to feel for others at times. Busyness, exhaustion, lack of boundaries, or painful life circumstances suck our compassion reserves dry. But I wonder how often something else is going on.

I recently came through an arduous season in my counseling practice. The downturn in the economy and financial instability pressed me into working more than my husband, Dave, or I wanted. And as much as I loved seeing my clients, the emotional toll of doing ministry, raising young children, and being a "professional" woman was fraying the edges of my soul.

One evening after working with some heavy client issues— like abuse, rape, grief, and chronic depression—I finished the night with a girl in her late teens. As she sat across from me, rattling through the petty woes in her life, my emotional exhaustion won. Usually I find myself relating easily to teenage drama; after all, most girls are only reacting to what they know. But on this day, I felt dead inside. I felt . . . nothing. I felt absolutely no emotion toward this darling little girl pouring out her heart to me.

My compassion meter was running on fumes. I'm used to feeling *something* toward clients, but my own stuff, my marriage stuff, was smack-dab in the middle of my counseling office, keeping me from feeling what I knew was my job—not as a counselor, but as a fellow human being—to feel, to relate, to empathize.

Here's the trouble with lack of compassion: God made us in his image, and one of the main ways he describes himself is compassionate. If God had a business card, I think he'd want "compassionate" listed right under "Supreme Creator of the Universe." He uses this word to describe himself all the time. He practically shouts it throughout the Old Testament: "I am gracious and compassionate, slow to anger and abounding in love!"² God: compassionate creator. Us: compassionate image bearers. Makes sense, right? And it doesn't stop there.

God took it one step further when he put on flesh and walked among us. In the New Testament, Jesus modeled compassion *with action*. When Jesus feels *splagchnizomai*, the Greek word for compassion used in the original text, he always does something about it. *Splagchnizomai*—a cool-looking word that I pronounce "splaag-nose-me" or "crazy-free"—literally means to feel it deep down in our guts for someone else. To be moved to nausea for other people's needs, as my pastor likes to say. That is some deep feeling. That is living life to the full, feeling and experiencing love and pain with others. Yet so often we are wrapped up in our own stuff, and we just can't feel for others the way God intended.

When things aren't settled or right in our souls, we are hindered in our ability to feel deeply and take action in love. Compassion is always a prerequisite to love. When we lack empathy, when we feel empty and numb, we need to take a clear, honest look at the issues that block our compassion and love for others.

Symptom #3: Convoluted conflict

Conflict is always hard, but heart issues make it even more painful. The difficulty of expressing feelings, the struggle to be heard and known, and the pain of compromise make everyone (except maybe trial lawyers) recoil from a fight with a loved one.

Last week I met with a friend who told me about a recent argument with her husband. My friend Liv is what you would term "low maintenance." She's a friend you'd love to have. She prides herself on managing conflict well at work, addressing things directly in friendships, and fearlessly taking responsibility for her own issues. So she seemed shocked by what she called "a swing and a miss" with her husband.

Liv explained: "I had just been thinking about how one of my employees—a single mom—lives on *half* of what I make. I started feeling bad about the way I spend money, like my pedicures and the clothes I buy my girls, and I felt like maybe I needed to rein in my spending. So over dinner I said to my husband, 'I think we need to do a better job managing our spending.'"

Liv leaned back so she could emphasize her point. "I was shocked by his reaction. All of a sudden, it was like I was talking from over here," she said, swinging her hands apart to illustrate, "and he was talking from way over there." Next she smashed her fists together and said, "Then we crashed into one another. We didn't talk the rest of the night."

As we talked and I asked some questions, I better understood why Liv called this "a swing and a miss." Liv's husband handles all the family finances, and he thought her offhand comment was a judgment call on his money management. They both overreacted to the actual conversation at hand.

But here's the real story, the conversation they *weren't* having. Liv is the family's breadwinner. Her husband is a stay-at-home dad. This creates all kinds of insecurity between them. That insecurity, when left unchecked, causes their disagreements to derail faster than a kindergartner trying to tell a joke.

Liv continued, "The conversation became so tense we couldn't even express what we were trying to say to one another. He was obviously upset because he thought I was criticizing him. I was upset and angry because I am freakishly insecure about money, my job, and whether it's right that I am a working mom. What a failure to communicate!"

Like it or not, conflict is going to be a part of all relationships—and the way we handle it can be a very good thing. Proverbs 27:17 says, "As iron sharpens iron, so one man sharpens another" (NIV). I can't read this proverb without picturing my university's athletes-only weight room. My fellow cheerleaders and I often worked out there next to the varsity football players. That little room in the basement of the basketball arena was so memorable—and I'm not even talking about the muscles! What I remember most is the constant sound of moving iron—clinking, clanging, slamming to the ground—and the hard work it took to move it.

The weight room—and the proverb—reminds me that iron clanging into iron isn't a gentle experience. We need the clang and the sharpening from one another to work toward resolution and to grow as people. But when we are stuck in our own issues, we often derail a conflict before we get close to the good stuff. Maybe, like Liv, we've had some communication failures—so we avoid conflict altogether and miss out on the chance to grow and change. Or maybe we've experienced so much hurt in conflict that we charge in like a lioness, claws unsheathed, lashing out at anyone who stands in our way. A tendency to either avoid or attack in conflict is a sure indicator that other issues are lurking.

WHAT'S NEXT?

Blindness about our issues, lack of compassion, and unhealthy conflict are three symptoms of a heart that needs tending. Although heart issues come in all shades and variations, in this book we'll explore five consistent problems. I've observed these issues over the past decade of teaching, counseling, and ministering to women of all ages. When I was first working with women, I would sit across from a client and think, *Wow! I'm not the only one dealing with this?!* After thousands of conversations, most around one of these five issues, I find myself wondering, *What woman* doesn't *deal with this?* Although the details of stories in this book have been changed, you'll probably find a lot to relate to from your own life too.

So welcome to the She's-Got-Issues Club—you're in good company! Here are the top five (drumroll, please):

- control
- insecurity
- comparisons
- fear
- anger (and its cousin, unforgiveness)

In the coming chapters, we'll cover these five ordinary issues that most women face. Most likely, you struggle more with one or two of them, but read about them all. Not only will you find shades of yourself in every struggle, but you'll gain compassion for friends who struggle with issues different from yours.

How to use this book

All you need to begin this journey is a willing heart, although having a Bible, journal, and pen wouldn't hurt either.

Each of the five key issues—control, insecurity, comparisons, fear, anger—is covered in two chapters: the first defines it; the second explores how to deal with it effectively. In the first of the two chapters, you'll find an assessment that will help you identify how intensely you struggle with that issue. Be honest with yourself while answering the questions—you'll find far more to relate to!

The second chapter in each section also includes a "Word Up" section, designed to allow you a time of focused attention on Scripture that speaks to that issue. If a story catches your interest, put this book down and pick up God's Word. Read the story or verse in your Bible, and the stories and verses around it too. God's Word has the supernatural ability to satisfy your longings in a way that no other word can, and I hope this book will be the first step in a long and exciting journey into the Bible for you.

Every section concludes with questions for personal as well as group reflection. I affectionately call devoting time to such reflection in my own life "taking a space bar."

Taking a space bar

Has it ever seemed to you like life is moving so fast that you are goingwithoutspacebars? Just as you can probably decipher the jumble of words at the end of the last sentence, most likely you can keep pushing through your crazy schedule—at least for a while. But just as words would eventually lose their meaning if there were never a space between them, so life lived without any spaces or margin comes to feel like a lengthy run-on sentence.

We human beings have an outstanding ability that sets us apart from all other creatures on earth. This is our ability to think about thinking, or what psychologists term *metacognition*. Thinking about our thinking is innate, yet when life comes at us fast, we often forget to do so. We don't take the space bar between relationships, circumstances, and emotions to look back and think. We don't think about the thinking that's driving the action that's driving us crazy.

Scripture instructs us, "Take heed to your spirit, that you do not deal treacherously" (Malachi 2:16, NKJV). Taking a space bar is our chance to take heed to our spirit, to pay attention to what the actions of our lives tell us about the condition of our spirit. It's only by paying attention that we can ensure we are not dealing treacherously with people and with God.

I've found three tools to use during my space bar moments to
help uncover the issues lurking in my heart:

- **An incident.** Think of a recent situation that didn't go
  the way you wanted, or of a problematic relationship that
  you spend a lot of time thinking about. Having a specific
  example in mind will help as you learn about yourself.
  What/who drives you crazy? What's a recent interaction that
  you can use as a case study? Some of the questions at the end
  of each chapter will help prompt this thinking.
- **Prayer.** It is rare that we set out to intentionally wrong
  another person or act unkind. So if you're in turmoil over a
  situation or a recent interpersonal interaction, keep in mind
  that you likely have already concluded that you are in the
  right. Ask God in a simple way to enter in with you to this
  space bar. "God, I know there is a way that seems right to me.
  Would you open my heart to receive your instruction in this?"
- **Writing on the why.** My counseling supervisor is known to
  say, "Journaling is the cheapest form of therapy." You must
  get out what has gotten in, and often writing is the best
  way to do so. Frequently people don't stop to think beyond
  whatever's frustrating them. Instead, they camp out on that
  thought and allow an endless and repetitive complaint to
  dominate their mind. Writing can help us get unstuck and
  move on to the final "why" of our actions.

  If I find my sister annoying, my natural response is to
  dwell on what annoys me about her, never asking the next
  question. Writing on the why is about that next question.
  It's asking myself in the space bar, "But *why* does she annoy
  me?" "What do I want to be different?" And then asking the
  next question, and the next, until I finally get to the rock-
  bottom statement of my soul, the place often visited by pride

or fear or self-centered desires. That's the place where we can be met by Jesus, our provider, our healer, our savior, our rescuer—the one who can satisfy us in our deepest place of need and direct us back into our lives with freedom and love.

This book will walk you right to the door of this last step, but it's up to you to walk through it with Jesus and into a place of true transformation. And it's worth making the journey.

You might consider using this book with a small group, women's ministry, or another friend. There is great freedom in transparency. My desire is that this book will invite you into that place of honesty, and if you take that plunge with another friend, the reward will be even greater.

A ground rule: please do not assess one another's issues! There is plenty of work for you to do on yourself, I promise. Instead, consider your small group or friendship a place where you can be a cheerleader—encouraging and affirming one another as you peel back some layers of plastic and ultimately discover the beautiful, authentic women God has made. The questions for discussion at the end of each chapter will provide a starting point for real conversation about your issues and God's work.

Now let's move on to the good stuff: our lives, God's Word, and the divine mystery of his transforming work in our hearts!

SPACE BAR

A PRAYER

God, I find my heart confusing! You know me far better than I know myself, but I know I'm not living the full and free life you've provided for me. Would you give me the strength to be honest with myself—and with you—so I can take the next step toward freedom? Amen.

A JOURNALING EXERCISE

1. Which of the following "ordinary issues" do you struggle with most consistently?

Control	Insecurity	Comparison
Fear	Anger	Unforgiveness

    Describe a recent incident in which that issue was front and center.

    _____

    _____

2. How have you seen these issues hinder your relationships? What circumstances make them visible to others?

    _____

    _____

FOR GROUP DISCUSSION

Do you feel like you have a faith testimony worth sharing? Have you ever experienced (or known someone who's experienced) *real* change through a relationship with Christ?

Nicole reveals the issues she struggles with most. Snap the code with your smartphone to watch this bonus video or visit the link below.

www.tyndal.es/ShesGotIssues1

CHAPTER 2

MORE THAN MEDIOCRE
(A.K.A. THE GREEN SQUARE)

We can only be used by God after we allow Him to show
us the deep, hidden areas of our own character.

OSWALD CHAMBERS

I HAVE A CONFESSION TO MAKE: I have a happy-ending addiction.

I love happy endings so much that I have a hard time getting into a new story without reading the ending first. I just have to know there will be resolution, things tied up in a bow, a satisfying "the end." And I'm not alone: a recent study tested readers to see whether they enjoyed a story more if it came with a "spoiler," if they knew how the story would turn out before they read it. And they did. Across the board, every kind of story—mystery or literary—was more enjoyable when the reader knew what was going to happen.[1] Apparently, I am not the only one who doesn't want to be kept in suspense.

But my addiction to happy endings is not limited to the page—it goes for life, too. I expend enormous energy trying to get to the endings, going for the quick solution even in complicated situations. My relationship with Jesus is no exception, and it all started with a wordless book.

SALVATION TICKETS AND HEAVEN SONGS

The wordless book was the pièce de résistance of every Good News Club and vacation Bible school of the 1980s. Genius, really: a matchbook-sized craft that fit perfectly into my grubby five-year-old palm. Five squares of felt, each a different color, stapled together to form a book that tells the ol' gospel story in easy-to-repeat steps:

Step #1: The black felt stood for my sin. A very dramatic beginning for any preschooler.

Step #2: Red for Jesus' blood, the payment for that sin.

Step #3: White felt for snow, a symbol of the forgiven sinner's squeaky-clean heart.

Step #4: Yellow for the golden streets of heaven, where I would one day walk (*if* I said yes to Jesus).

Step #5: Green, springy, and new, my new life of growing(!) and thriving(!) and blooming with God(!).

Simple enough. The book was so short I didn't have to flip to the end, plus they had me at "golden streets." At the tender age of five, I said yes to Jesus in my neighbor's kitchen. I repeated the sinner's prayer (another set of steps) after my leader. She celebrated while I smiled down at the beige and white linoleum, singing about my happy ending with all the little boys and girls on Lamb Court (the actual name of that street—the irony has not escaped me):

Heaven is a wonderful place,
Filled with glory and grace!
I wanna see my Savior's face 'cause
Heaven is a wonderful place!

I liked knowing the ending, and as we sang that song, I pictured golden candy wrappers, My Little Ponies, and maybe that Barbie Dream House with the elevator. I conveniently forgot that the heaven square wasn't actually the end of the book, that saying yes to Jesus wasn't just about a salvation ticket, and that the yellow square didn't represent happiness here on earth.

The wordless book was just the beginning of my Christianity confusion. My entire spiritual history is full of five-step promises for happiness, feeding my conclusion addiction. Fast-forward a couple of decades, and quick-fix solutions still fill bookstores. If I had never heard of Jesus and tried to figure him out based on the books written about him, I would think he had quite a bit to say about dating, dieting, medicine, dress codes, politics, leadership, parenting preschoolers, and caring for aging parents. I would think he was prone to talk about guidelines and steps.

SERIOUSLY, WHY ARE WE HERE?

I've spent most of my adult life talking to people about relationships of all kinds—about the fearful-of-commitment boy, the attention-seeking sister, the soul-sucking mother-in-law. I listen to people talk about themselves and the ways they fear and fail in relationships. I've been educated in all kinds of solutions when it comes to healthy and happy relationships. My favorite DIY cure is "short-term solution-focused therapy." Doesn't that sound promising? Pair "solution" with "short-term," and I'm sold. That's exactly what I'm looking for—something to fix problems and not take too long doing it!

As much as I'd like to believe in short-term solutions, my own spiritual life hasn't worked that way. I wanted my Christianity to begin on Lamb Court—but maybe I also wanted that "yes" to be the happy ending. But somewhere between my bad perm in seventh grade and year two of marriage, I realized that the end goal of my faith—the fuzzy yellow square that promised streets of gold—wasn't getting me my Barbie mansion or my Cabbage Patch Kid or even a fulfilled life with a side of Jesus. I felt betrayed. I felt like I had failed. I thought I had followed the steps, and God wasn't holding up his end of the bargain.

What I forgot was the green square—the square about growth. I'm not sure what kind of growing I expected, but I certainly didn't think it would take much time or work or (noooo!) pain.

I didn't realize that I couldn't hold up my end of the bargain—the loving-others part—without a real, vibrant, living, *growing* relationship with Jesus. The green square that I had overlooked for years finally caught up with me, and it taught me more about heart care and true life in relationships than my counseling degree and all that self-help required reading had.

Happy endings aren't a myth. Jesus really *is* the happy ending I've been looking for. The ol' gospel I heard at age five is still good news, but I'm finally getting that knowing Jesus isn't just about salvation, it's about the work he can do to change you *as a person.* Don't miss the importance of that line. Knowing Jesus is about allowing him to make you new, to create in you a pure heart, and to develop your passion for him and for others. It's about trusting him to shape your life and fashion you into exactly the woman he intends. Whether your issues are lifelong or circumstantial, they are the very place where God wants to begin the work of growth and change.

To follow Jesus is to agree to change. That's the cost required of us. We care about changing because God demands it. Here's the great thing about God's demands or "law." As our Creator, he knows what will bring us the most joy and the fullest expression of his presence while we are on earth. The commandments he sets in place for us are actually *for our good.*

Moses, when giving his final sermon, repeatedly tells God's people that choosing God's way is choosing *life* (Deuteronomy 30:15-16, 19-20; 32:47). That's life in the fullest sense—thriving and abundant.

I love that Moses even tells the Israelites to write down God's law as a song (Deuteronomy 31) so it will be easy to remember that staying within God's boundaries is the way to thrive in this life. Once we get a taste of that, when we understand that following God's demands leads us to our deepest desires, we won't want anything less.

There is no way to follow Jesus' call without an inside-out transformation of your heart.

But our hearts are stubborn and we like to do things our own way. So before we get into each specific issue that hinders us from the free life, let's talk about the three premises of change that form the basis of this book. These are the starting point, the foundational truths that will lead us into the deeper places of growth.

Premise #1: You are crazy (at least a little bit)

It was getting late on a Sunday night and I was cleaning up the church kitchen after the atomic bomb that is youth group. Several high school girls hung around, swinging between counters and perching cross-legged on tables. "Okay. I have this crazy thought," said Olivia, like she had just discovered the cure to cancer. "I think you are always the weirdest person you know."

I just kept wiping the counter because I needed a bit more explanation. She started to laugh, a big, full laugh that's contagious. "Nicole, you know what I mean because I know you are weird!"

I've been working with the teen girls in my church for more than a dozen years, and doing life with them has always been a great adventure. For the months leading up to that evening, Olivia and I had spent a significant amount of time together, long enough for us to let our masks come down and to share our real hearts. In the process, our own "weird" was uncovered. I know she struggles with fear, and she knows when I get obsessed with control. As we get honest with ourselves and others, we make a discovery. Call it weird, or crazy, or broken, or messed up. But we can't go anywhere until we call it. *We are all a little bit crazy.*

Crazy people are no strangers to the Bible. Look no further than King David for an example. As a young Israelite, David rises to fame first by killing Goliath the giant and then by gaining infamy in King Saul's inner circle. He is not afraid to collect two hundred foreskins, the price to marry King Saul's daughter. (All right, King Saul might be the weird one here.)

Saul's admiration of young David turns to bitter jealousy, and Scripture follows Saul's attempts to hunt down and kill David. The story gets even weirder. Once, while King Saul is chasing David down, Saul stops to "take care of some business" in a cave. It happens to be the cave where David's hiding. He could kill Saul, but instead he sneaks up behind him and chops off a corner of his robe. Crazy, huh? It's like a taunt. David appears to be invincible. Years pass. David rises to prominence and even becomes king after Saul's death, experiencing unprecedented success and favor for Israel.

At this point in the story, you are probably wondering what's ordinary about this guy. And so as painful as it is, I'm glad God included the next part of his life. The part where David, in the height of his influence, makes some stupid choices. While strolling along the palace roof, he sees a beautiful woman (Bathsheba) and has to have her. He summons her, sleeps with her, impregnates her, and then tries to cover up his mess, given that she's the wife of his good friend and warrior Uriah. David brings Uriah home from battle and tries to get him drunk so he'll sleep with Bathsheba before he goes back to war. When Uriah doesn't follow the plan, David arranges for him to be killed in battle. Yep. The harp-playing, poetry-writing, dance-worshiping, giant-killing, warrior-king David in one of the worst displays of self-ishness and sin ever recorded. (This is all in the Bible!)[2]

It's hard to even wrap my mind around that experience, but the Bible doesn't just leave us David's history—it provides us with his own words, written at all stages of his life. In the Psalms, David pours out his heart; one day full of distress (Psalm 5), the next full of awe at God's majesty (Psalm 8). He worries that God has forgotten him (Psalm 4). He laments his sorry condition after the Bathsheba incident (Psalm 51). He's depressed. He's elated. He trusts God, then he worries. He's angry. He's sorrowful. He's anxious. The whole of his experience is, well, crazy. And oh. so. real.

In the story of David, we find every aspect of the human condition, every emotion of the heart. In the Psalms, David lives inside out, throwing open the door of his heart and mind—and encouraging us to do the same. He looks honestly at himself and leaves us an example of the incredible results of facing our issues head-on. After all, David is remembered by God—despite his sin—as a man after God's own heart (Acts 13:22).

Can you imagine being named by your Creator as a woman after his own heart? And if David is an indicator of qualifications, clearly we don't need to be perfect or even "good" to be what God is looking for. "Crazy" doesn't disqualify us from God's favor. I think honesty (in our crazy) is vastly pleasing to God.

Premise #2: You can't fix yourself

When I was running my counseling practice, I would begin my first session with clients by asking, "Can you tell me what prompted you to call for an appointment?" I wanted to understand the exact circumstances that led to their tipping point, the moment when they knew they needed some help.

Most had little problem explaining the reason they'd come to see me. At subsequent meetings, however, I often noticed that although they were willing to get help from me, they felt either that their problem was too small or that they were too unimportant for God to deal with.

We've heard it said that no problem is too small for God. On an intellectual level, we accept that. Yet on a heart level, we often resist asking God for help unless we are teetering on the edge of life's cliffs. Maybe we think God has bigger concerns to deal with. Maybe we're afraid he won't show up for us. Maybe we think we should just try harder. Maybe we know we often create our own messes, so we assume we should clean them up.

I recently came across a journal I kept when I was twenty-three. Like an oracle to my future struggles were these words, written in my own hand: "I guess since I made this mess, I don't think I need God to help me out of it." Regardless of the reason, too often we resign ourselves to the ache of the ordinary rather than accepting the truth that we aren't strong enough to change by ourselves.

I often wonder if that desire to change ourselves without God's help is just pride disguising itself as weakness. I'm no Bible scholar, but there's a consistent theme through Scripture, and it most certainly isn't "God helps those who help themselves"! Rather, the theme of Scripture is that God helps those who need his help— he helps the humble: "I will bless those who have humble and contrite hearts, who tremble at my word" (Isaiah 66:2).

So what exactly is humility? Sometimes it's easier to know it by what it is not. Humility isn't about downplaying your strengths or depreciating your worth. It's not pity or an aw-shucks patronizing view of yourself. Humility is about knowing the truth about yourself and your proper standing with God. Humility is accepting that you are weak, that your heart is beyond your own understanding. Humility is acknowledging that you have a Creator who knows you better than you know yourself. Humility is knowing this reality: "I decide to do good, but I don't really do it; I decide not to do bad, but then I do it anyway" (Romans 7:19, *The Message*). Humility says, in every circumstance: *God, I need help.*

God's answer? He *likes* humble people.[3] He promises to guide, save, sustain, and give grace to the humble.[4] Those are promises that bring transformation.

Premise #3: God can transform you

God can, and God will, help you deal with your issues. *If* you let him. This is the sticking point. Even if you can accept the fact that he can solve your problems, you may not be ready for complete surrender. You may even have to admit that the idea of turning over control to God makes you want to say, "God, thanks but no thanks!" In Isaiah 55:8, God says, "My thoughts are not your thoughts, neither are your ways my ways" (NIV), which sounds like a guarantee that he's not going to change you according to your plan. And while you are being honest, perhaps you wonder if a "relationship" with God can actually help you at all. Keep reading, and see what he can do with even the tiniest shred of faith!

Step one is admitting you have a problem. Remember the printout exercise I described in chapter 1, the one where I asked you to consider how you'd feel if all the thoughts you've had in the past week could be captured on paper and then printed out for your friend or pastor to read? Do you have peace about the way you love others? Me neither. So . . . can you admit, at least to yourself, that you have a problem?

Step two is realizing you can't solve that problem. I want you to think about one of these common issues (comparison, insecurity, fear, control, unforgiveness, anger) and ask yourself: *How long have I struggled with it?* My guess is that most of us would say it's been years. So if you know something's not good for you but you've struggled with it for years, you have to admit that you aren't doing very well on the solution side of things. So . . . can you admit, at least to yourself, that you haven't been able to solve your problem?

You must accept these two realities if you want to reach for the next—that God is willing and interested in meeting you at these issues and using them to change you.

WORD UP

At the beginning of his Gospel, the disciple John tells us something crucial for our understanding of this transformation that is both birthed and blessed by God:

> To all who received [Jesus], to those who believed in his name, he gave the right to become children of God— children born not of natural descent, nor of human decision or a husband's will, but born of God. The Word became flesh and made his dwelling among us. We have seen his glory, the glory of the One and Only, who came from the Father, full of grace and truth. . . . From the fullness of his grace we have all received one blessing after another. (John 1:12-14, 16, NIV)

First, note that God's way is a rebirth. When I was five and saying the sinner's prayer, I had no idea what rebirth really meant. As an adult who grew up in church, it's easy to skip the words *born again* because I've heard them so many times. If that describes you, stop for a moment and think about the idea of being reborn. If you've given birth, you probably have all kinds of associations: pain, mess, drama, joy—but certainly birth takes *work*.

This change in your heart, this rebirth, is accomplished "not with a physical birth resulting from human passion or plan" (John 1:13). It is neither your will nor your planning that makes this happen. It is not the strength of your ability to say no that makes you a child of God. It is only your utter dependence upon him, your complete rebirth into his way that will change you.

When we decide to follow God, we choose a whole new way that is independent from our own ability to plan or purpose or muscle our way into being good. God isn't working in our issues to make us need him less. He's interested in moving through our issues so we can understand just how desperate we are for a constant inflow of his love into our hearts. This isn't about perfection, about *being better*; it's about *being changed*—reborn, remade every single day into the likeness of Christ. Remember David: like him, we won't be perfect, but we can be women after God's own heart.

John goes on to tell us that from this rebirth, given by the grace of God, we receive blessing after blessing. What is a blessing? The source of all "truth," Wikipedia, says that a blessing is "the infusion of something with holiness."[5] In other words, a blessing is like a shot of God in your life. Imagine yourself being infused with the divine. If you've ever received intravenous medication, you know how quickly it can affect you. Within seconds, a change comes over you as the medication courses through your veins. Now imagine that feeling representing the way God blesses you. Imagine an infusion of deep, abiding peace. This shot of holy love makes your heart beat fast, full to overflowing with grace and compassion for those around you. Doesn't that sound almost magical, to be so filled with *love* that you respond and serve—out of freedom, not out of obligation or manipulation or to feed your ego?

Of course that sounds amazing. Of course you and I would say yes to that kind of blessing. If it were that easy, this would be a very short book! But it's not so easy, and you need to continue to explore—with God, with yourself, with your small group—just what keeps you from living a fully infused, fully reborn life. This is what it means to be sanctified by God, and it's not a five-step process. It's an entirely new way of thinking, feeling, acting, and relating that requires giving your whole life over to God's rule.

On a scale of 1 to 10, how willing are you to let God be in charge of this process? This is a very important question. Along with the "God doesn't care about my small problems" excuse, I've often heard this: "I prayed for God to change [my husband/my friend/my situation], but he didn't. So I'm on my own." Too often we want God to work in our timing and in our way.

Our intentions for what we want might be pure, but we don't like God's method. We'd rather pray for God to change our husband than to give us patience. We'd rather God give us the first job we apply for than increase our trust. We'd rather have the relationship now than surrender to God's timing. So we pray for our husband to change, for the prospective employer to say yes, for the boy to ask us out. Our way. Our time.

Oh, friend, this is one of the main hindrances to believing in answered prayer! Praying for God to change specific things is like signaling a spaceship from your yard with a miniflashlight. "Follow my flashlight!" you shout as you wave your arm wildly. "I know what I'm doing!" The spaceship can see where it's going much better than you can. It isn't surrender when you pray for God to change somebody else. True surrender starts with arms outstretched and an open heart that cries, "*Do what you will.*"

Even if you must honestly say you are only a 3 out of 10 on a willingness scale, God will work with that. Change always, always begins with honesty. Give him your 20 or 30 or 60 percent surrender and watch him work it into something more. By the end of this book, my prayer for you is that your surrender and trust in him will be far beyond what it is right now.

Remember that God is not interested in transforming us because he needs us to be shiny, happy people who robotically do his will. He's interested because he loves us too much to leave us wallowing in our issues, mired in the everyday and missing out on his presence and peace! As Hannah Hurnard writes, "Love is beautiful, but it is also terrible: terrible in its determination to allow nothing blemished or unworthy to remain in the beloved."[6]

You are loved. You are worthy. And so you will be changed.

SPACE BAR

A PRAYER

Dear God, I'll be honest. I want your direction but often don't want your help. But I'm tired of doing this on my own. I've tried to fix myself and it's not working. So I'm going to tell you today, and tomorrow, and the next day—take me on. Mold me into the woman you want me to be. Open my eyes to the chains that bind me, so that I can allow you to break me free—to experience full, free, growing love for you and for everyone. Amen.

A JOURNALING EXERCISE

1. Can you imagine being described by God as "a woman after his own heart"? In what ways do you feel that's true? In what ways do you feel far from that?

   _____

   _____

2. Can you admit that you have a problem—a consistent, worn-out, not-going-away problem? Finish this thought: "I would describe one of my heart issues as . . ."

   _____

   _____

3. How have you tried to solve that problem? What's worked? What hasn't?

   _____

   _____

4. On a scale of 1 to 10, how willing are you to let God be in charge of this process?

_____

_____

5. Can you relate to any of these objections to God's work in your life?

      "My problem is too small."

      "I made this mess myself."

      "I've asked for God to change things, and he hasn't."

FOR GROUP DISCUSSION

1. Think of your own one-word associations with the word *birth*. How does the idea of being reborn sit with you?

2. Before reading this chapter, what was your understanding of the word *blessing*? What do you know of blessings from Scripture? What would you call blessings in your life?

3. Have you known someone who seemed "infused by God"? If so, what are some characteristics of that person?

Nicole shares three warning signs that indicate you've got issues. Snap the code with your smartphone or visit the link below.

www.tyndal.es/ShesGotIssues2

CHAPTER 3

I'M NOT CONTROLLING
(I JUST LIKE MY LATTE EXTRA HOT)

This is the stuff that drives me crazy. . . .
It might not be what I would choose,
But this is the stuff you use.
FRANCESCA BATTISTELLI

WHEN I GO INTO STARBUCKS, I want my order to be just right. I prefer that my latte be made with one percent milk, two shots of espresso, and two shots of vanilla. I like it low foam and extra hot. But that's a little what you might call high maintenance, so I restrain myself from asking for all five at once!

The same invisible force that nudges me to test the barista's memory—and patience—is at work in you right now. The force determines what you say and how you say it. It is the crayon that colors your past and will write your future. It is a complicating factor in your relationships with God and other people. And it requires constant tending. Yet my guess is that you've never thought very deeply about how this force works, when it formed, and where you really stand with it.

That force?

Control.

We talk about people being control freaks when they try too hard to manage others. (Given my confession about my detailed latte preferences, you may have already correctly pegged me as one.) Some people think there is a right way to do things, and I happen to be one of them. Sometimes it works out: I'm right and things go according to plan. But because life is more gray than black-and-white and because my internal rules don't come anywhere close to my reality, many times I am wrong.

At the other extreme, we call people "out of control" when they do a poor job of managing themselves. They frustrate friends and family members by their refusal to take responsibility and work toward positive change. Their understanding of control is completely different from mine, but it can result in just as many issues.

Another word for control is power; namely, the power we have over the course of our lives and over people in them. And why does this matter? Because my guess is that you, like me, have no idea exactly how much you are supposed to control. Too much control and we coerce and manipulate, thinking this is how we love people. Too little control and we abdicate our own influence and responsibility to be a loving force in the world. A misuse or misunderstanding of our own control is the issue that drives women crazy—crazy with exhaustion trying to manage every detail of life, or crazy with discouragement about the futility of life. What is our responsibility and what is not? What does God require from us, and what is he going to do himself? How exactly do we love someone without controlling him or her? And is there a way for us to understand God and our actions with a healthy view of control?

THE ORIGINS OF CONTROL

Let's begin to answer these questions by considering three factors that determine our own relationship with control:

1. **Our relationship with control is fueled by our beliefs.**
   Beliefs are our *rules for life*. They are often unspoken and
   sometimes unrecognized. They are the fuel that determines
   our actions and our feelings. You may have no idea why you
   get irritated at certain things your sister does or feel so much
   compassion for the homeless, but even when your feelings
   seem irrational, there's a method to your madness.

   Here's an example: For years I would find myself irritated when our garage needed straightening. I didn't know
   why, but I'd grumble under my breath whenever bikes were
   askew or the floor needed sweeping. I remember once coming in with a grocery bag on one arm and the baby carrier
   on the other. I stepped over a kid's toy and laid out a litany
   of complaints about my husband. Aloud. To myself. While
   kicking that kid's toy. I was irritated at both the messy
   garage and my husband, but I had no idea why.

   One day, while talking in a Bible study about belief
   systems, I made a discovery: I believed that cleaning up
   the garage was my husband's job. Humor me—I have no
   idea why I didn't recognize this earlier—probably because
   I was too busy kicking bikes and cursing. But my dad had
   always cleaned the garage in my house when I was growing up, so I naturally assumed that my husband would be
   the one to do the same in our house. Of course, I never
   told him that—I didn't even realize I had that expectation!
   But that invisible rule had power over my attitude and my
   emotions.

2. **Control is inextricably tied to our understanding of God's
   work in the world.** Have you ever thought, *My life is spinning out of control*? Just the use of the phrase betrays your
   thoughts about God's authority.

Perhaps "out of control" is easier to say than "God's in control," especially when bad things happen to good people, when natural disasters kill thousands. Perhaps your theology doesn't have room for a God who is, in fact, in control, even in the most brutal circumstances.

The phrase "My life is spinning out of control" betrays our belief that if we're not in control, nothing (or no one else) is.

I do not take this topic casually. Whenever I am in a room of more than twenty women, I know at least one of them has suffered some kind of abuse at the hands of another. To say "God is in control" to a woman who is wrestling with a true taste of evil in her life is like giving a Band-Aid to someone who just had a leg cut off.

So often we come up against trouble, large or small, that leads us to believe that God is not in control, or that he has forgotten us, or that he's punishing us. But Scripture tells us that God does not treat evil lightly. The prophet Jeremiah blasted the "religious" of his day who gave out these kinds of Band-Aids: "They dress the wound of my people as though it were not serious. 'Peace, peace,' they say, when there is no peace" (6:14, NIV). God does not treat our wounds lightly. He does not hand out Band-Aids like a school nurse. He is a surgeon—a healer. He treats our past, present, and future with great care—more than we could even imagine.

When you struggle to reconcile your troubles and God's role in them, don't despair. Dealing with your issues has an incredible result: beauty. Elisabeth Kübler-Ross, a psychiatrist specializing in death and suffering, wrote, "The most beautiful people we have known are those who have known defeat, known suffering, known struggle, known loss, and have found their way out of the depths. These persons have an appreciation, a sensitivity, and an understanding of life that fills them with compassion, gentleness, and a deep loving concern. Beautiful people do not just happen."[1]

The beauty that results from our trouble is one of God's great scandals—who but he could trade our ashes for beauty, could make his power perfect in our weakness, and could cause everything to work together for good?[2]

However, as we work through this struggle, we acknowledge that our thoughts about control become what we believe about God—and our view of God is what we project into our own relationships. Take Julie: as a young girl she witnessed her sister severely injured in a car accident. She's never reconciled where God was in that pain. And she doesn't let anyone drive her children anywhere. Our view of God's control is knotted together with the view we have of our own control.

3. **But most of all, control is about our sin nature.** Sin includes anything we do that separates us from a relationship with God. And control—how much is ours, how much is his—is so often linked to this sin nature. The proverb that begins with "There is a way that seems right to a man" continues "but its end is the way of death" (Proverbs 14:12, NKJV). Whoa. In a stark sentence, we see reality. We all have a default way of handling our lives, but this way has no life in it at all.

So often we think of sin as outright bad behavior—we use the Ten Commandments as a list of "things I don't do," like steal, murder, or commit adultery. But Jesus brought a whole new order to that checklist of rules when he told us what we *should* do by putting love first. Loving is something none of us do perfectly (or even well). Picture someone in your life who is hard to love. What would make him or her easier to love? My guess is that you think, *If they would just do X or act Y, then I could love them better.* You see, even in our love we exert control!

We don't choose the circumstances that make us feel out of control—but we do choose the way we react. Because of sin, we often choose self-centered options as the way to escape or change our reality.

Our ways might seem like a good option, but the important truth is that they're ours. And as we discussed in chapter 2, God's Word makes it clear that our ways do not equal his ways. God says, "My thoughts are completely different from yours" and "my ways are far beyond anything you could imagine" (Isaiah 55:8).

To those who argue with him, he answers, "Yet you say, 'The way of the Lord is not right.' Hear now, O house of Israel! Is My way not right? Is it not your ways that are not right?" (Ezekiel 18:25, NASB). God sounds downright indignant in this passage, and I can't blame him. Who are we to tell him how to do something when he's the one who created us?

God has a way. And it's not our way. His thoughts are completely different from and beyond our own. In that case, what hope do we have? Before you throw up your hands about ever making a right decision again, take in this promise from Isaiah 30:18-21:

> The LORD still waits for you to come to him so
> he can show you his love and compassion. For the
> LORD is a faithful God. Blessed are those who wait
> for him to help them. O people of Zion, who live

in Jerusalem, you will weep no more. He will
be gracious if you ask for help. He will respond
instantly to the sound of your cries. Though the
Lord gave you adversity for food and affliction for
drink, he will still be with you to teach you. You
will see your teacher with your own eyes, and you
will hear a voice say, "This is the way; turn around
and walk here."

What good news in the face of our own sin! What a promise
God gives us about his intricate and intimate relationship with
us! Rather than desperately seeking to control or passively ceding
all control, we are invited to a deep place of contentment that
balances our responsibility with God's grace and guidance. When
we find this place, we will neither try to dominate the world nor
be helpless victims. This middle place isn't free from pain, but
it is full of peace. And it's worth the work to find it! In the next
chapter, we'll break down how this passage can instruct us in a
God-centered concept of control, but first, let's begin to look at
where our beliefs begin.

CONTROL: HISTORY LESSONS FROM LIFE

I once had a client, Sophia, who insisted that every door and
window in her house be locked at all times, even if she was just
going out into the driveway to retrieve something from her car.
For Sophia, the world is a scary place, and being a lock dictator is
the only way she feels control. I feel for Sophia because I know this
behavior stems from many factors, such as her temperament and
her parents' overprotection. She seems to fear that the one minute
the house is left unlocked, kidnappers will jump out of the bushes
and steal her children, but even control over this minute possibility does not contribute to a comfortable inner world.

What Sophia has a harder time seeing is that her issues with control shape the world around her. When she yells at her husband to lock up (for the sixth time), when she runs back to the door to check it again while her children watch her from the living room, she's passing on her issues to the next generation. The very thing she's trying to control is really controlling her.

This is the bitter fruit of believing we are in control. The apostle Paul says we are either "slaves to sin" or "slaves to righteousness" (Romans 6:6, 18, NIV). He doesn't offer a third way, contrary to popular culture's promise that, as an independent woman, you'll have freedom! Rather, "you are a slave to whatever controls you" (2 Peter 2:19).

Why is this important? Because your issues with control aren't a passing trend. When you try to manipulate and control a situation or relationship, you are operating out of a well-worn pattern, something that began in the womb, was shaped through childhood, and is reinforced in your adult life. Often control is the factor behind why you think, act, and feel in ways that seem irrational and unpredictable. Not only that, but the issue of control—where it comes from and what it does in your life—is often an umbrella issue, one that casts a shadow not just over you but on those around you. Loving others is harder when your primary concern is maintaining command over your own circumstances.

While Sophia desperately tried to keep herself and her family safe by controlling her environment, fifteen-year-old Emma tried to keep the peace in her relationships by ceding control. Emma called me and asked if we could meet to talk about some "friend issues" she was having. When we met, she explained to me the problem.

"Maddie's been my friend since kindergarten. We grew up together; she's practically my sister. And we have been best friends for a long time, but lately things are harder . . ." Emma trailed off, twisting the cap of her soda bottle on and off. "She can't stand it if I go out without her. There's a new girl at school that I just became friends with, and Maddie invites herself along when we go out. If I tell Maddie I don't want to spend the night with her, or I just want to stay home on the weekend, she tells me that of course I want to come over, and before I know it, I'm saying yes."

Loving others is harder when your primary concern is maintaining command over your own circumstances.

Drink forgotten, Emma continued, "Sometimes it's like I have no idea how to think or feel when I'm with her. And if I do just ignore it, she'll text me or make fun of me on Facebook, and then tell me it was just a joke and I should be a good sport. When I call her out on it, Maddie goes from being mad to teary, and I end up comforting her instead of confronting her!"

In this example, it's easy for us to see the problem: Maddie is controlling. Something is driving her to want to control this friendship, and until that comes out into the open, Emma is going to continue to be miserable and misunderstood. Maddie and Emma are in a friendship where control is out of whack. Maddie has too much control, and Emma doesn't have enough. And *both* of them are to blame.

Both girls are operating from a complex set of variables that contribute to their beliefs about themselves and their perception of how they are to operate in this world. Although Maddie might drive to control the relationship, Emma also contributes by giving in to that controlling behavior. Most of us tend to relate to either Maddie's or Emma's way of dealing with relationships.

So how does the way we express control affect us? How does our understanding of why our life is the way it is matter? What difference does it make why we feel unsafe or refuse to take risks, or why our friend's passivity bothers us so much? Because as we wrestle with these questions, trying to make sense of it all, we determine the course of our heart and our actions for the rest of our life.

My pastor once told me that he believes every woman becomes either beautiful or bitter by the time she's forty. What he meant was that women either face their stuff or they don't. Women make choices either to do whatever is necessary to keep as much control as possible, or to work hard to understand what is in their control and what must be entrusted to God. If they face it, they heal, they forgive—they tend to radiate an inner beauty that reflects Christ in them. That beauty is accessible to every woman and has nothing to do with the color of her eyes or the size of her jeans. If women don't face their struggles, they become bitter—holding on to their issues and spewing them onto other people like germs.

I see the potential for both in my own life. I see it in the high schoolers I hang with, in the twentysomethings who are making life decisions, in the new moms struggling with identity.

There is another choice for women who don't face their issues. They can become beaten. A beaten woman is one who's been knocked out by life and hasn't ever recovered. She's given up on her childhood dreams of love, of fulfillment, of purpose. She tends to be the woman who's always helpful and "nice" but never really known. I have met many of these women. They stay in the corners. They smile widely but cower quickly. Each one has a story of what snuffed out her light, and every one of them makes me sad. Their way of controlling life is to give up everything about themselves for whatever they want to protect. Their only control is self-protection, figuratively throwing the covers over their God-light and just surviving. They feel like pawns in the chess game of life, always being shoved by some invisible force, living out a part in someone else's game, just trying to stay alive.

Each of us has a choice as to how we will respond to what life brings. Kind of goes back to that same proverb . . . do we choose our way and death, or God's way and life?

ASSESSING YOUR CONTROL ISSUES

What about you? Do you usually seek to control the situations and people around you, or do you act out of the belief that you actually have very little control? Are you most like Sophia, Emma, or Maddie?

To help you dig into your own beliefs and to make this chapter personal to your life today, I invite you to take the following assessment. There are no right or wrong responses to any of the statements. They are simply like shovels you can use to dig into the dirt of your life, to get down to the foundation and discover where you might want to do some repair work.

ARE YOU A CONTROL FREAK?

Think back over the last few weeks, and then answer each statement with a "T" for mostly true or an "F" for mostly false. You can probably think of some exceptions to either answer, so just go with your first instinct.

_____ 1. I try not to plan too far ahead or get my hopes up because I can't predict how things are going to turn out.

_____ 2. I often think, *If you want something done right, you have to do it yourself.*

_____ 3. I believe that if I work hard enough, the majority of the time I'll get what I'm after.

_____ 4. When I've figured out a certain way to do things, I like to tell people, because everyone wants a faster and more efficient way to get things done.

_____ 5. Capable people who fail haven't taken advantage of every opportunity.

_____ 6. I often feel frustrated that life isn't going my way.

_____ 7. I often feel that what is going to happen will happen.

_____ 8. People would say I have a stubborn streak.

_____ 9. I prefer the driver's seat (literally and figuratively).

_____ 10. Other people's messes bother me.

_____ 11. Many unhappy things in people's lives are out of their control.

This assessment offers you just one tool to help you evaluate your understanding of control. Consider your responses as you consider how you perceive control and what you can do about it.

CONTROL SETTINGS

Control is a goal from the moment we are born. As soon as the umbilical cord is snipped, we begin the journey toward independence. We first exert that independence as children learning to do things ourselves, and mastery over our environment is a crucial stage in human development.

As we've discovered, our beliefs about life, our understanding of God's work in the world, and our sin nature help form our beliefs about control. Yet how we approach control and mastery is shaped by multiple other forces as well, including our personality; our environment, specifically our parents' way of loving and disciplining; the dynamics with our siblings; and our culture. Researchers also say the amount of control people feel toward the world is tangled up with their "worldview" (a.k.a. religion), further proof that how we view God and his domain affects us at the deepest level. All of these factors make for a complicated mix.

Your beliefs and experience have given you what psychologists call either an internal or external locus of control. If it's internal, you act based on the understanding that you need to maintain a firm grip on your world. You are a king. If external, you feel the reins of control are held by someone or something outside you. That makes you a pawn.

Pawns and control

In her friendship with Maddie, Emma exhibited the traits of a pawn. If you agreed with statements 1, 7, and 11, you may relate to her.

An external locus of control has become an important measure of personality theory for everything from mental illness to academic success. A person with an external locus of control is likely to attribute life events to things that are impossible to influence, like fate. This person tends to think, *I can't control that* in every area of life.

Childhood trauma, regardless of the severity, is a huge factor in how you view control. If you felt unsafe because you were violated physically, sexually, or emotionally, you are likely to not feel in control. Something happens to us at the deepest level when we lose that sense of mastery over our own space. (Thankfully, there is a God who can handle even that, who is able to restore us to a sense of our own mastery, which we'll discuss in the next chapter.)

Personality often contributes to the development of pawns as well. They generally take life as it comes, making them more likely to be flexible and spontaneous, less likely to be orderly and scheduled. That approach to life isn't wrong, but it does help determine how you will feel about your level of control.[3]

In our performance-driven culture, an external locus of control isn't exactly heralded. Yet there's a part of this preference that's not bad. Such people are more likely to be laid back and certainly are less likely to try to manipulate situations for their gain. On the negative side, people with an external locus of control are more likely to be stressed and depressed.[4]

Kings and control

If you agreed with statements 2, 3, and, 5, you may have an internal locus of control, and your relationship with control is more likely to be that of a king. In other words, you are likely to think, *What happens to me is my own doing.* Across the board, those with an internal locus of control tend to take more responsibility for their actions, have a greater sense of influence, and are more likely to take care of their health.[5]

If you are king-oriented, you likely see that you have a great amount of control in this world. You tend to understand how your actions can influence others and how you must take responsibility for your own life. On the other hand, you are likely to bump up against some opposition as you explore the boundaries of your control. Like a person who touches an electric fence, kings generally end up being "shocked" when they encroach into an area they discover is not actually in their domain.

Not enough control creates a victim mentality and steals our joy. Too much control creates a lack of flexibility and steals our joy.

Perhaps you planned your wedding—every last detail but the groom—before you left middle school. And you've been shocked to find that despite your best attempts, the groom hasn't shown up on time. Or maybe you fantasized about what life would be like once you had the house, the husband, and the kids—and it's nothing like what you pictured. You operate under the conviction *I can control the outcome of my life*, but your reality begins to disagree. This is where we struggle with our own kingship.

One approach to reconciling the mismatch between our beliefs on control and our reality is to *try even harder* to control everything. My world doesn't feel safe, so I'll *try even harder* to make it safe by becoming more vigilant. My groom doesn't arrive on time so I'll *try even harder* to make sure I find a man to date. My career isn't as fulfilling as I thought so I'll *try even harder* by switching jobs (again). Webster defines a control freak as a person "who has a strong desire to control others and situations around them." Add a tendency to kingship with strong expectations in life, and you might be prone to some control freakiness (statements 4, 8, 9, and 10).

In addition to personality, past experiences also play a role in our views on control. Nothing seems to bring out the control freakiness in women like a breakup or a baby. Some of the craziest stuff I've ever heard from others (or done myself!) involves women and their broken hearts. How I cringe when my young friends confess checking their ex-boyfriends' e-mails and Facebook or doing daily drive-by stalkings as they try to make sense of why their love has left them! These women are so good at undercover investigation that they should sign up to find America's Most Wanted! The betrayal, shock, and loss of a breakup sometimes drive them to crazy things.

That same intensity seems to be the fuel behind new-mom angst. In the first few months of life with Charlie, my oldest, I went from fun-loving youth leader to Nazi-mom. I had lists and charts. I had schedules and routines. I had times when the dog could bark and times when that wasn't allowed. I had "times when Charlie can be picked up and held" schedules. I don't know how anyone survived being around me!

I love young moms so much, and I empathize with the wild look in their eyes as they try to figure out how to protect their infant from the baby-eating monsters that lurk around every corner, looking for yummy babies to wrestle out of their mothers' arms and eat for breakfast. I'm thankful for that mother instinct because in many cases it is the catalyst that helps women embrace a new understanding of control, of God, and of his work in their lives.

WELCOME TO THE HUMAN CONDITION

While our temperament definitely plays a role in our relationship with control, many personality theorists point out that we are not likely to be either fully "external" or fully "internal" in the way we view control. And most likely that's true for you. There are probably some areas where you feel very much in control and other areas where you do not. (If you agreed with statement 6 in the control assessment, that may be particularly true.) But what I've discovered is that my relationship with control instructs me on some deeper issues at hand, particularly pride (*I don't want this, so I'm gonna change it!*) or fear (*I am scared of this so I will avoid it*). Fear and pride are often the deeper motivators behind our control issues.

Fear says, *I must do these things so that nothing bad happens.* Fear can drive normal women to turn into crazy mothers-in-law who instruct their daughters-in-law on every single aspect of how to raise a baby. Fear is what drives the teenager to stalk her ex-boyfriend on Facebook. (*What if I end up alone?*) Fear is what causes Sophia to freak out on her husband when the door is unlocked for sixty seconds (*What if we get hurt?*).

Pride also exerts control. Pride says, *I know how my life should go.* Pride says, *I deserve this.* Pride says, *This is what should come my way.* Pride is a secretive force behind so many of our control issues, and it's a chameleon. Pride disguises itself as common sense and knowledge and hard work. But it's a dangerous creature because of the insidious ways it penetrates our heart and attempts to keep us king of our lives. We often accept perfectionism in our lives, another way pride disguises itself. That excessive preoccupation with doing things the right way stems from our deep belief that we know the right way, we can do it the right way, and life should go our way because of it.

Because life does not exist in the black-and-white, we recognize the pawn and king in each of us. There are times that pawns, or as Judith Viorst calls them "surrenderers," need some more "get up and go." There are times when kings, or control freaks, need a little more "sit down and shut up."[6] But what we all need is the space and courage to honestly face our beliefs about control.

At a recent staff meeting, our youth team broke into groups

to take a space bar from the hectic pace of life and to pray for one another. We each confessed what hinders us in our relationship with God. Howard, a former football player who resembles a teddy bear (and if teddy bears had hearts, they would model them after Howard's), confessed his inability to give up control.

"I just go about 80 percent of the way and then I don't give it all up," he said. "What can I say? I think I know how things should go; I want to do it my way. I want God to be in control, but then I don't want him."

Next to him, a young twentysomething nodded. "I'm the same way," she said. "And I know that God wants my full surrender."

Is there anything more difficult that yields a sweeter result? We must crucify ourselves—our agendas. We must give up our rights to ourselves—our plans. We must lay it all down before the true King—and ask him to have his way. The result is a sweet freedom. We discover that the control we have so desperately wanted has actually kept us chained and paralyzed. We recognize that we are certainly helpless sheep who thrive only with a strong shepherd. In the great paradox of freedom, we find life by giving our life to Christ.

SPACE BAR

A PRAYER

God, whew! I have issues I didn't even know about. And control is a big one. Would you equip me with the ability to know what's mine to handle . . . and the strength to trust you with the rest? As I begin this journey, I say with the psalmist: "Investigate my life, O God, find out everything about me; cross-examine and test me, get a clear picture of what I'm about" (Psalm 139:23, The Message). Grant me the courage to open my eyes to how control keeps me from loving you and loving others, and the strength to trust that you actually do hold all things together. Amen.

A JOURNALING EXERCISE

Review your control assessment. Take one or two of the statements and expand them into a written prayer. For example, you might say, "God, I know I have a stubborn streak. I tend to see things my way and want people to get in line. . . ." Use those revelations as a prompt to confess to God the parts of you that want to manage life apart from him.

_____

_____

_____

_____

_____

FOR GROUP DISCUSSION

1. When it comes to personal achievement, do you have a king or pawn tendency? How about in relationships with others? with God?

2. What areas in your life do you tend to overcontrol? What areas do you tend to undercontrol?

Nicole speaks on how much—or how little—we really allow God to be in control. Snap the code with your smartphone or visit the link below.

www.tyndal.es/ShesGotIssues3

CHAPTER 4

SURRENDERING
THE KUNG-FU CONTROL GRIP

The greatness of a man's power is the measure of his surrender.
WILLIAM BOOTH

MOST OF MY FAMILY thought it was a game, but I secretly considered it a weapon of mass destruction. It was a long-standing trick between all of the siblings to subject one another to "tickle torture"—but it felt more like a gang initiation to me. The basic premise: tickle someone until they pee or surrender. In her diabolical mind, my sister began to think "tickle torture" was a great way to wake me up, and unfortunately for me, my favorite sleeping position was with my arms straight over my head.

I hated surrendering. I hated having someone make me say or do anything I didn't want to. And so I clamped my arms down by my sides. I ignored my impulse to get into my comfortable sleeping position, waking myself up throughout the night and shifting position, putting those arms back down at my sides. I trained myself out of my natural sleep state so I could ensure that I would not be tickled.

I think we sometimes learn to control our faith in the same way. If we come to know Christ as a child, we start off with a legitimate childlike faith. We fling our arms up in surrender and trust his way.

But we get tickled, or tortured, or both, into a place of realizing that we have to control this life if we are to avoid painful or uncomfortable situations. We begin trying to manage and manipulate situations to our liking. We clamp our arms down by our sides and refuse to get back into the vulnerable and childlike state of arms-wide-open surrender.

Jesus says, "I tell you the truth, anyone who will not receive the kingdom of God like a little child will never enter it" (Luke 18:17, NIV). If you're thinking, *How will understanding the Kingdom of God break me out of my control freaky ways?* slow down and trust me. (Get it? Surrender!) Or if you have spent most of your life trying to meet another person's demands and keep him or her happy, you might wonder, *What role could I possibly have in God's Kingdom?* I can assure you, God has a place for you. Because when you begin to understand his Kingdom, you see with your own eyes the truth: that surrendering completely to God is the key to the full and free life.

CONTROL: A NEW DEFINITION

Do you know that God actually made you a ruler? Not as in a straight-line producing tool, but as in, well, a princess. I've actually never been a big fan of the princess-in-God's-Kingdom analogy. It is just too fanciful, and when I'm unloading the dishwasher for the third time in one day or realizing that I'm the one who's going to scrub out the ripe trash can, I don't exactly feel like a princess.

Princess or not, the Kingdom of Heaven concept is Jesus' go-to phrase. He's constantly comparing the Kingdom of Heaven to tangible examples on earth to help us understand . . . examples like treasure in a field, yeast in dough, pearls lost, seeds sown, and a party thrown. It's a concept that's so central to his teaching and so clearly about our present-day life that we must pay attention. The concept of rulership is also a theme throughout Scripture and is an essential part of our understanding of our lives on earth. So let's take a look at what exactly the Bible tells us about our role in rule.

Truth #1: We were made to rule

In the very first chapter of the Bible, God describes life as it was meant to be. He created man but didn't leave him to laze around naked eating grapes all day. He assigned him a role here on this earth, and that role was to rule. We get a peek into the world of the first and perfect loving relationship, Father, Son and Holy Spirit,[1] as they discuss the creation of mankind in Genesis 1:26: "Let us make people in our image, to be like ourselves. They will be masters over all life."

The original Hebrew words used to describe the "masters" are forceful, almost violent. God gives us the innate desire to rule our environment, to "take charge!" as *The Message* version of this passage says, of all the earth around us. This is good news for control freaks. God designed us to want to master the world around us. In fact, Psalm 16 tells us we are assigned a portion by God as our inheritance.

> LORD, you have assigned me my portion and my cup;
>   you have made my lot secure.
> The boundary lines have fallen for me in pleasant places;
>   surely I have a delightful inheritance. (verses 5-6, NIV)

This is the concept of our own kingdom—the influence in our lives that God has given us to manage.

So what's the problem? The problem is that God's original design was that we would rule alongside him in an intimate, devoted relationship. Within that context of loving relationship, we were given freedom to rule our domain, whose boundaries would be set by God. Our childlike trust of his perfect rule would color everything we experienced in this life. We would respond to him and then carry out his will in our "kingdom" or area of influence.

But when Eve and then Adam disobeyed God's rule, everything changed. In one moment of disobedience, they usurped God's rule. They used the incredible gifts God has given humans and exercised them apart from his boundaries. I can identify with Adam and Eve. There is a pull within me that wants to run things by myself. There is a stubborn streak in me that wants to set my world in motion all by myself, that believes I truly know what is best for myself. It is the part of me that wants the world to rotate around me—my needs, my whims, my desires. This force has been kicking in me since I was born. And it's not dead yet.

But one of the best and hardest lessons I've ever learned is that I'm not the center of the universe. If only things happened when I wanted, people responded to me the way I desired, and all of life operated on my timetable! If only I maintained my patience, if only others understood my deepest needs, if only I didn't mess up! Doesn't that sound just perfect? Perhaps like paradise, even?

Of course, I make the assumptions that Eve did on that idyllic afternoon in the Garden. I assume that my perspective on life, my filter for people, my intelligence and grossly limited understanding of the way the world operates is enough. I make some pretty outrageous assumptions, considering myself as the center of the universe, and when I stop and think about it, it's pretty crazy. But sometimes I don't know how else to run my life except my way, with me at the center. So what is the alternative?

Truth #2: Our influence aligned with God's influence =
unstoppable power

Women, hear me when I say this in love: we have control issues because we believe we are the center of our universe. We come by it naturally, and we've been dealing with it since our ancestor Eve evaluated a decision apart from the will of God. Often we don't stop to really consider how our innermost beliefs about control affect our behavior. Yet in many ways, our attempt to direct events betrays the truth of our hearts, *even when we want good things for ourselves or others.*

When you take time to think about control, I would guess that you feel exhausted in your desire to spin things your way. That you are tired of holding up your life and everyone else's. That the mask you wear to show you've got it all together has worn thin and you are having a hard time keeping it in place. Good news—you are approaching the Kingdom of Heaven.

Jesus said, "Blessed are the poor in spirit, for theirs is the kingdom of heaven" (Matthew 5:3, NIV). You are blessed—you are moving toward God—when you realize that you have been far from him. You are blessed—moving toward God—when you feel like a spiritual failure. You are blessed—moving toward God—when you realize that the lie of your independence has left you lacking. Another version translates this truth, "You're blessed when you're at the end of your rope. With less of you there is more of God and his rule" (*The Message*).

Do you feel exhausted in your desire to spin things your way? Good news—you are approaching the Kingdom of God.

When Copernicus theorized that the earth was not the center of the universe, as had been believed, he introduced a dramatic paradigm shift that affected everything anyone had thought about the earth. Instead of the earth being the center of the universe, it was part of a vast but organized array of planets and stars. Instead of occupying a unique place in the universe, Copernicus said, the earth orbited around the sun.

All of us need to embrace our personal Copernican revolution: recognizing that we aren't the center of the universe. Choosing to be satisfied with our positioning, orbiting around the Son. Choosing the freedom that comes when we realize it is not our job to control everything and everyone in our lives. Choosing to embrace our place in the story and follow Christ's lead rather than passively wait for events to happen. Oh, relief! Once we get past the sting of repositioning, we recognize the joy that is ours just by doing what God has given us to do. We give him back what he has given us so abundantly—our strengths, our gifts, our resources. We take what he has given us—our kingdom and our rule—and we align it with *his* Kingdom and *his* rule. We stop feeling the friction and gravity of living out of his celestial alignment. We realize that we play a small but crucial part in his plan. We are neither all-important nor meaningless in his universe. All we have to do is get aligned and let him do the rest.

Truth #3: Choosing to lay down our kingdom is a lifelong event

Wouldn't it be nice if we could just get this right once and for all, and then never think of it again? I would love to know and recognize my own rule, align it with God's rule, and then see what happens. I would love to never struggle again with knowing how much to say to another person, when to exert my opinion and when to stay quiet. I'd love to know when to let my kids make bad choices and when to stop them. I'd love to know when to confront a friend because I'm hurt. I'd love to know when to tell my husband that he needs to do something differently. I'd love to know when to "speak the truth in love"[2] and when to let "love cover a multitude of sins."[3] I'd love to know how to be right without needing anyone else's help.

Wait . . . I'm back in my kingdom! I'm fully controlled by my need to control. Because if I knew all these things, I'd be the center of the universe again, leaving God's orbit and creating my own. Do you see how even good motives lead me to independence? How my well-intentioned desires to do things right lead to my sin-nature-intentioned desires to live my life apart from God? Maybe this is why Scripture continually points me back to my proper positioning before God, as his child.

When David cries out to the Lord, he positions himself not as a powerful or strong warrior-king but as a little child. In Psalm 131:1 (NIV), he says, "My heart is not proud." He knows he should not concern himself with "great matters or things too wonderful" for himself. Instead, he chooses to become still and quiet, using the imagery of a toddler being rocked by his mother.

Can you imagine yourself becoming still with your Lord, who rocks you against his chest? This is a picture of utter dependency, and it's a daily choice. Each day you can take your concerns and lay them on your Father God's chest, resting in this quiet place. You can be rocked by the One who knows you better than you could ever know yourself, who loves you more deeply than you can fathom, and who holds the whole world in his hands. This is our great God, who spins the earth on its axis and yet tenderly, gently offers us the image of a nurturing mother to describe his care for us.

When you don't know how to deal with your boss, when you want to manipulate a situation in your favor, when you can't stand the customer service representative for your cable TV, when the whole day seems turned against you, when your toddler screams, when your dog gets loose, when you don't get the job, when you don't like your life, when you wonder if there's any sense to it all—listen for God's quiet reminder: *Be still. Humble your heart.*

Lower your head. Rest in my presence. Rest in my Kingdom. Rest in my love. Accept my embrace. And trust like a child.

What if we ordered our relationship with control from that same perspective—not as sophisticated modern women but as children? What if we tried to sort it all out into some simple truths, statements we could carry with us, written on our hearts, and through which we could filter our decisions about how we look at our lives and interact with others?

That would mean, first, that we recognize those things we do not control. (By control, I'm referring to the things we can predict the outcome of with 100 percent accuracy because we are fully in charge of the decision.) For instance, I made the following list of things I can't control:

> the length of my life
> other people's actions
> natural disasters
> my child's temperament
> my physiological needs (sleeping, eating)
> my family of origin
> my childhood story
> my level of intelligence or physical strength
> my height
> my skin color
> the speed of the driver in front of me
> my children's school experience

I'm confident you could add hundreds of things to this list. In fact, if you focused only on what you could not control in one day, you might wonder if you truly have any "rule" on this earth at all!

But just as important is realizing what *is* within our control.

What is 100 percent within our ability to effect? My choices for that list would include

> my posture toward God's Kingdom in my life
> the space I make for God
> the way I treat God's Word
> my attitude toward others

Can you think of any others? I struggled to come up with more items for this list. I'm reminded that, like a child, I am not in complete control over very many things. Yet those that I'm given to control are crucial!

God will orchestrate your circumstances, which may include sorrow and joy. He will continually and relentlessly present his love and his Kingdom to you—but he won't force his way in. He won't make you choose him. He leaves this, the most important aspect of your life, up to you. So what is your posture toward God's Kingdom in your life? Can you explain his role and his rule? Do you believe that he is both present and active in your life? That even when hardship comes, he can—and will—work all things together for good? Scripture tells us story after story about how we should view our control—but I'm partial to Joseph's.

WORD UP

Joseph's story occupies a whopping fourteen chapters in the book of Genesis, giving us a rare glimpse into a prolonged portion of this man's life. At first glance, the story of Joseph reads like an action adventure, beginning with his betrayal at the hands of his envious brothers, his superhero-ish ability to interpret dreams, a desperate situation that throws the country into turmoil, and the ultimate prospering and prevailing of Joseph (happy ending!). Except—that's not how Joseph seems to view these events. Joseph consistently removes himself as the main character of his own story—and squarely places that control in God's hands.

After being stripped, thrown into a pit, and then sold into slavery by his brothers, Joseph experiences an incredible turn of events, and he finds himself prospering under the authority of one of Pharaoh's officials named Potiphar. But there's trouble in paradise. Potiphar's wife goes *Desperate Housewives* on Joseph and attempts to seduce him. He turns down her proposition—not to honor Potiphar, but to honor God. "How then could I do such a wicked thing and sin against God?" (Genesis 39:9, NIV).

With these words, Joseph acknowledges that his choices here on this earth directly affect his relationship with God. He understands that when he makes choices—good or bad—he ultimately has to answer to God's rule. Thrown in prison after being framed by Potiphar's wife, Joseph has the choice to become bitter about his "pawn" status in this game of life. Yet he persistently puts the control back in God's hands while managing what he should: his actions and his beliefs. He attributes both good and bad to God, but with a trusting attitude.

When given the chance to interpret dreams for the cupbearer and the baker for the king of Egypt, Joseph quickly attributes his ability to interpret as belonging to God. Even when the cupbearer is released from prison but forgets his promise to plead on Joseph's behalf, Joseph maintains a sense that God is the main character in his story. He is imprisoned for two more long years—more time to wait, to trust, to surrender. And when finally brought before Pharaoh and given the opportunity to interpret a dream for him, Joseph doesn't wrestle control back from God. He once again says, "I cannot do [the dream interpretation], but God will give Pharaoh the answer he desires" (Genesis 41:16, NIV).

When Joseph ultimately prospers under Pharaoh, he does not forget who is in control, despite his rise in prominence and position.

He names his children Manasseh "because God has made me forget all my trouble" and Ephraim "because God has made me fruitful in the land of my suffering" (Genesis 41:51-52, NIV).

Joseph finally meets up with his brothers again—the same ones who betrayed him and sold him into slavery—and he interprets his life with a God-informed perspective. "It was to save lives that God sent me ahead of you" (Genesis 45:5, NIV). Can you imagine what it would be like to stand before someone whom you had so blatantly betrayed? Back in the fields near Shechem, Joseph's brothers thought that selling Joseph into slavery was taking care of a problem that had plagued them their whole lives—their father's blatant favoritism toward their cocky younger brother. But now many years have passed. Sorrow and suffering have visited each of the brothers. Their own poor choices, made in the spirit of their own "rule," have played out poorly (see, for instance, Genesis 38). Yet in a strange twist of events that can only be attributed to God's hand, Joseph now stands before his brothers and proclaims, "It was not you who sent me here, but God" (Genesis 45:8, NIV).

After caring for his brothers and their families and being reunited with his beloved father, Joseph continues to prosper as a chief official in Egypt. Yet even though Joseph has shown mercy, his brothers' faith still falters. When Jacob, their father, dies, the brothers wonder if Joseph has truly forgiven their grievous sin. "What if he bears a grudge?" they murmur to each other. "What if this was all a show for Dad?"

Perhaps they themselves have not experienced the transforming power of God's love enough to know that it can truly cover their sin. They throw themselves down before Joseph, much like the wayward young man who returns to his father in Jesus' story of the Prodigal Son in Luke 15. The brothers of Joseph—and the wayward son of Jesus' tale—have nothing left to offer but themselves. They surrender all to the person in power, offering themselves as slaves and completely abandoning all control of their own lives. And both Joseph in Genesis and the God-figure in Luke 15 respond with love. Joseph buries the hatchet once again, reminding them that it was God who took what they intended for evil and made it good.

Talk about control! Can you believe that God can take even what was intended for evil in your life—and actually use it for good? That God can take that which causes you pain—and turn it into joy? God promises us "beauty for ashes" (Isaiah 61:3), continuing this theme of the great economy of his love. And Joseph is a reminder of the truth of that promise. Despite a life that seems out of control and with many opportunities to claim power for himself, Joseph consistently chooses to posture his heart toward God.

When good comes, he believes God has blessed him. When evil comes, he believes God can transform it. His perspective is always informed by his belief that God is in control. In turn, he is able to extend grace to others, even those who have hurt him deeply. In his commentary on Joseph's life, Matthew Henry says, "Make your peace with God, and then you will find it an easy matter to make your peace with me."[4]

THE PRACTICE OF SURRENDERING TO GOD

Joseph models a surrendered life. If we want to face up to our "issues" that stem from control, we must follow his example. Remember, this is not a one-time thing. A surrendered heart and life require constant upkeep. The natural tendency of the heart— if left unchecked—will move us toward independence. So the practice of yielding ourselves, of discovering our inner little child, is one we must cultivate on a daily basis.

Surrender as a posture

Surrendering to God's way is the only way to true, vigorous life. The idea of surrender found in Hebrews 12:5-9 is all about the training and disciplining that a loving Father provides his children.

> "My child, don't make light of the LORD's discipline,
>   and don't give up when he corrects you.
> For the LORD disciplines those he loves,
>   and he punishes each one he accepts as his child."

As you endure this divine discipline, remember that God is treating you as his own children. Who ever heard of a child who is never disciplined by its father? If God doesn't discipline you as he does all of his children, it means that you are illegitimate and are not really his children at all. Since we respected our earthly fathers who disciplined us, shouldn't we submit even more to the discipline of the Father of our spirits, and live forever?

My favorite moms to hang out with are the ones who provide their children with loving, consistent discipline. I love hanging out with them because I love their kids! Although our children's temperaments are not in our control, the need for discipline borne out of love is familiar to every mother.

The practice of yielding ourselves, of discovering our inner little child, is one we must cultivate on a daily basis.

Likewise, the author of Hebrews draws the parallel between our own surrender to discipline and God's loving rule. We submit because it leads to life: "Since we respected our earthly fathers who disciplined us, shouldn't we submit even more to the discipline of the Father of our spirits, and live forever?" The Greek word for "live" in this verse is *zao*, which is defined as being among the living (not the dead!); as having true life; as being fresh, strong, efficient, powerful, active, and full of vigor. Jesus uses this same word when he describes himself as "living water," "the bread of life," and "the resurrection and the life."

This is the kind of life for which Jesus suffered and died: "For the joy set before him he endured the cross" (Hebrews 12:2, NIV). Jesus endured betrayal, beatings, and death—and counted it all *joy* because he knew that he would be the gateway to real *zao*, real life, for everyone who believes in him. This *zao* offer, this gift of life through Jesus' death, was not accomplished easily. And though it costs us nothing, it certainly cost Jesus dearly.

Jesus' life on earth, his death, and his resurrection, were not just some sort of cosmic reset, a reason to endure this life and hurry up to heaven. Rather, his life was about restoring us to the Father's love. And it is only in our full surrender to God's way of doing it that we encounter this true, active, fresh, vigorous *life*.

These truths must become the backbeat of every move we make. Imagine these truths as from the drum in a band, beating out a rhythm that every other instrument responds to. The drumbeat is the anchor that keeps the melody from floating away. And this is the drumbeat that keeps us in a posture of surrender and allows us to begin to open our hands to God's way.

My pastor has a saying that leads us all back to this point of surrender. Whenever we, as a staff, feel overwhelmed by the needs we can't meet, the complaints we can't soothe, or the people we can't appease, he reminds us: "There's a Lord for that." When the relationship fails, *there's a Lord for that.* When my child is unhappy at school, *there's a Lord for that.* When tragedy strikes, *there's a Lord for that.* When discouragement clouds, *there's a Lord for that.* This simple phrase reminds me that there is a Lord, a ruler over all, and that is not my position. I don't have to hold it all together or give it all up. I can surrender to his plan and then be obedient to just what he calls me to do. When I surrender to his way, my drumbeat becomes "There's a Lord for that." For every situation, big or small, Jesus Christ is in control.

Surrender as a habit

In describing submission, author Nancy Guthrie says, "Whatever God allows to happen, we can give ourselves over to his goodness."[5] There is a discipline to believing that God holds all things together. In the book of Job, we must wrestle with the reality that God truly is sovereign over all—even our suffering. In one catastrophic swoop Job loses his children, his fortune, his strength, and his health. And as he clings to life and to his tenacious belief in accepting both good and trouble from God's hand (Job 2:10), we discover a secret to the practice of surrender. In his misery and waiting, in his distress, in the buzzing flies of his friends' bad advice, Job continues to come to God honestly. He pours out his heart and his lament, yet he keeps God in his position of authority. God does not want our submission to be that of a cowed puppy, ears down, whimpering in his presence. Rather, our surrender comes in a shout or a whisper or a cry that says, "I give you all I have, and I accept what you give. Even when nothing around me looks good, I'm believing you are still—and always will be—good."

This is a daily need for my life. Every morning I need to check my heart to see who's ruling. I would like to say that I leave God on his throne, but it seems like most of the time I'm playing king of the mountain. Wrestling my way up his leg, trying to work my way into his seat. And I believe my Father God chuckles at my antics and lovingly returns me to my place. Just as it should be.

Surrender by check-in

Surrender is also a learn-by-doing activity. Oh, how I wish I didn't have so many opportunities to check my control freakiness!

My most recent opportunity came during our drive to church. Everyone who has tried to get more than one person out of the house for church knows that more cajoling, strength, and stamina are required on Sunday mornings than any other morning in the week. The mad dash for coffee, shoes, lip gloss, and keys is combined with the effort to round up the kids and get them finally wrestled, er, secured in their car seats. This week, we finally got ourselves into the car, running about five minutes late. Now, church is only about seven minutes down the road, but these are crucial moments that determine how much time I will have to chat before worship begins, which is clearly an acceptable thing to be concerned about if I am the center of the universe.

As my husband drove us down Patterson Avenue, I felt a rising tide of anxiety. My internal dialogue sounded a little like this:

We can't possibly be driving close to forty-five miles an hour.

(Glancing over at speedometer) *Great. We're going forty-seven. Way to push the limit.*

(Drumming my fingers on the armrest) *Seriously, I think a dog just passed us, running faster than this car is moving.*

(Tapping my foot, drumming my fingers, and checking the speedometer again) *Apparently we're going to the eleven o'clock, not the nine-thirty service. At this pace we're guaranteed a spot at the five o'clock p.m.*

As I forced myself to look out the window rather than punch my husband's leg into pressing the gas pedal, I found myself in a surrender check-in. Is a thirty-second delay in our church arrival time worth a bad attitude? Worth a tense ride? Worth picking a fight? Is my rising anxiety really about this ride or about the sitting in the passenger seat of life? And as I ruminated on these thoughts, I arrived at the reality that plopped on my heart like a rock: *Just whose interests do you care about?*

The mental space bar allowed just enough room for me to put my finger on the real truth. Were my thoughts about speed and our car ride about my husband's interests or my own? Because if I were loving him well (or at all), if I were putting him first, I would relax and enjoy the ride. I would honor his way, his timing, and his speed. There's just no other way to cut it.

I've found this question helpful to consider as I navigate the turbulent waters of giving direction to young people in my life—my children as well as the students and twentysomethings I'm around in ministry. When I find I'm particularly passionate about a point I want to make or a direction I think their lives should head, I try to stop myself and think: *Do I want this turnout for them or for me? Is this about me looking good or somehow justifying my own life choices? Do I want to empower them for this answer because I've prayed and listened to God or because I'm exerting my own right to rule?*

The beautiful thing about the practice of surrender—the posture, the habit, and the check-in—is that it allows us the confidence to use our influence as God intended. As we make peace with our controlling habits, we are more aware of the God-given influence that we truly have.

Surrender by acting on our God-given influence

In God's great exchange, he uses our complete surrender to bring us to places of greater influence. As he draws us into a childlike relationship with him, we begin to turn to him as the source for all direction. And as he whispers "This is the way,"[6] as he always has, our hearts are quiet enough to hear him. "Gentleness . . . will mean experiencing genuine brokenness and a crushing of self, which will be used to afflict the heart and conquer the mind."[7]

TEMPTED TO CONTROL?

When you find yourself tempted by a desire for control, take a space bar to determine the real motivation behind your behavior. Ask yourself:

- Why am I trying to control or influence this situation?

- Have I earned the right to be heard? Am I the only one who can speak into this person's life?

- Am I demonstrating daily my surrender to God? Am I living Isaiah 30:18-21 (see page 69)?

- Do I struggle with being a pawn? If I'm living my life with a victim mentality, am I making sure I use my God-given influence?

- Do I struggle with being a king? If I'm living with the desire to control too much, am I evaluating whether I should use up some of my influence by exerting myself in this situation?

If you struggle with control, the idea that God has afflicted your heart and conquered your mind might not seem that awesome. But sister, I am praying that as you look directly into your own motives, as you invite your Savior into the deepest parts of your soul and the most tenacious roots of your beliefs, and as you give him the right to reign in those things—you'll discover how present he really is in the smallest details of your day.

My youngest son is just learning how to swim. As he becomes more comfortable with his skills, he paddles farther away from me. But he makes eye contact with me regularly and frequently. Even underwater, his chubby little hands flap toward me and his eyes remain fixed on mine. When we surrender control, we are learning to swim in a whole new ocean. We exert our influence and share our lives with others, but we constantly make eye contact with our Father God, keeping in check with his positioning, knowing that we want to be within his easy reach.

Remember the passage from Isaiah 30 that we first looked at in chapter 3? These verses bring life to God's promise that his blessing comes when we allow him to reign in our lives:

> The LORD still waits for you to come to him so he can show you his love and compassion. For the LORD is a faithful God. Blessed are those who wait for him to help them. O people of Zion, who live in Jerusalem, you will weep no more. He will be gracious if you ask for help. He will respond instantly to the sound of your cries. Though the Lord gave you adversity for food and affliction for drink, he will still be with you to teach you. You will see your teacher with your own eyes, and you will hear a voice say, "This is the way; turn around and walk here." (vv. 18-21)

We must instruct our hearts to believe the promises of Isaiah 30. If we believe what God offers here, we will experience change in the DNA of our souls. God promises that he will respond regularly (verse 18) and instantly if we wait for him (verse 19). Difficult situations do not mean he is absent (verse 20), and he will respond specifically to our requests (verse 21). Help doesn't get any more practical than that!

In God's great exchange, he uses our complete surrender to bring us to places of greater influence.

As we put a surrendered life into practice, we will begin to notice something. Change in our character creates changes in our behavior. We become gentler with the unexpected and unwelcome intrusions into our life. Our hearts become softer and we make peace, even with pain. We respond to others with compassion and grace. The chains of fear and pride fall away, and we become childlike in our trust of God's hand in our life.

It is not easy work, but it is rewarding on the deepest level. Once we get a taste of the change God can work in our lives, when we see what he can actually do when we wrest control out of our own hands and place it in his, we will want more. Even when the crushing of our hearts feels excruciatingly painful, the joy and beauty that pour out will make it worth the work.

As we fix our eyes on Jesus in every decision, we will also experience our influence growing. "The eyes of the LORD search the whole earth in order to strengthen those whose hearts are fully committed to him" (2 Chronicles 16:9). In the private moments of surrender, we become strengthened for the public arena of our influence. We earn our right to be heard by others, not because you and I have great advice or because of our intelligence, but because our character is changed by a surrendered spirit. As we give up our own control to manage life and others, we will discover that God gives us incredible influence.

How do you know if you've earned the right to be heard? People will begin to ask you questions. They will want you to speak into their lives. They will offer to give you the very thing that you had the hardest time giving up—control! Because of the gentleness and humility that are born out of surrender, others will be drawn to you.

Let's take the example of my friend who has to lock all of her doors all the time. Imagine if she begins to surrender her life, the good and the bad, to God. What if she takes a space bar every time she checks the locks in her house, so that she realizes she is driven by a constant, gnawing fear. She gets honest with God about that, pouring out her heart and listing out every fear. She allows him to intervene and hears a couple of gentle whispers, small but compelling, that grow her faith. As she feeds her faith and continues to take space bars in her fear, she begins to believe in God's intimate involvement in her issues.

As her spirit becomes softened by God's work, her husband and friends notice something different in her. They become intrigued by the change. At first her husband doesn't say anything, but the atmosphere in the home is different. Where he felt tension, he now feels joy. My friend's influence doesn't come through Bible knowledge or the right words. Her influence grows as a result of her surrender and the change in her character. She begins to earn the right to be heard by her husband, and he becomes more willing to respond to the needs that drive the fear that created her controlling attitude toward locking the house.

At times you may be unsure of how much influence you have with someone and whether you have earned the right to be heard. Perhaps you love them deeply and want to see good things for them, and you are concerned about choices they are making. Maybe this person is your teenager, or your young adult son or daughter. Maybe this person is that college roommate you have kept in touch with. It could be a person with whom you used to have great influence but now you aren't so sure.

My pastor once told me that influence is like a poker game. You and I earn our chips as we grow in character and confidence. With every person we influence, we have a certain number of "chips" that we've worked to gain from them. It is not an infinite amount, and every time we exert our influence over them, we trade in our chips. If we exert our control over a weighty matter, it will cost us. If we exert our control over a smaller matter, it will cost us.

The illustration reminds me that my influence is not infinite. That every time I choose to speak into someone's life, I am cashing in some chips with them. It doesn't matter if this person is my child or my spouse! Even then I must earn my right to be heard, in the way that I care for them, the space I make for them in my life, and the love that I show. And even then, when I exert my influence, I cash in chips.

The way we wrestle with control, the way we use our influence for God's purposes, and the way God increases our influence in response to our surrender is a lifelong process. This is where an issue becomes an asset. The more we pay attention to our own tendencies to be a king or a pawn in life, the more likely we are to experience God's loving but firm hand, molding us into women who live in the truth that God has it *all* under control. We can give him our everything and know that he'll use every last shred, good and bad, enabling us to channel his love and compassion in our spheres of influence. This, friends, is what it means to live in the Kingdom of God, even on *this* side of heaven.

SPACE BAR

A PRAYER

God of all creation, it's amazing to think that you made me in your image. It is an incredible honor to think that you designed me to rule in this world and to use my influence to be a force for your Kingdom. I want to lay down everything you've given me and reaffirm that it's all yours. Would you teach me to wait when you tell me to wait, to speak when you tell me to speak, and to act when you want me to act? Holy Spirit, I pray that my spiritual ears will be open to hear your voice and to follow your lead. In Jesus' name, Amen.

A JOURNALING EXERCISE

Now that you've identified some places of control in your life, let's make it personal and practical. Make a list of some people and situations that you are tempted to control. You might want to start with acknowledging your desires for certain situations and people (e.g., I wish Jill was more interested in our friendship). What do you need to do to turn them over to God?

_____

_____

_____

FOR GROUP DISCUSSION

1. Can you think of a specific time you've surrendered yourself to God? What situations draw you to surrender?

2. Read Isaiah 30:19-26. Where do you need to trust God to respond regularly, instantly, and specifically in your life?

3. Have you experienced God using trouble to teach you? What did you learn?

4. How are you at "earning the right to be heard"? With whom do you need to use more words? With whom do you need to use more actions?

Hear from Nicole how surrender can free you from control issues. Snap the code with your smartphone or visit the link below.

www.tyndal.es/ShesGotIssues4

CHAPTER 5

INSIDIOUS INSECURITY

Enough about me, let's talk about you. What do you think of me?
C. C. BLOOM, *BEACHES*

FROM THE OUTSIDE, it looked like any event that brings women together—a bridal shower, a book club, a college reunion. With shoes kicked off, feet on the sofa, the women in the room were what the world would describe as elite. College graduates, some with advanced degrees. Attractive. Fit. Affluent. In many ways, they embodied exactly what the world tells us women strive for: the perfect home, the perfect husband, the career, the children. Not to mention the leisure time to sit with feet kicked up, enjoying a glass of wine and laughing with friends. The whole scene was perfect enough for a catalog picture, a snapshot of women living securely in who they are and what they've accomplished.

Except.

Except that we had gathered to pull back the covers on our true insecurities and expose every way that this picture-perfect circle of women is anything but. Our hostess, Melissa, confessed that she didn't even want to have us over because her house isn't decorated and it's quite small (in her opinion). Fran talked about living every day in a world she didn't expect—after her husband lost his job, they'd had to move out of their dream home and in with her mother (*gasp!*). Jessica, in her young twenties, confessed how difficult it is to be in the in-between stage of life, where she is neither married nor a mother nor a college student nor, well, anything that she wanted out of this season of life.

I sat behind my computer, tapping out thoughts on my keyboard until finally I had to sit back and just take it in. How did we, such powerful, beautiful women, ever become so insecure? And as evidenced by our passionate confessions and convictions, how could we move into a place of true security in the gritty reality of a life that hasn't turned out as expected?

Before I began writing this chapter, I had a hard time defining insecurity. It's a cloudy kind of word, with all kinds of associations and feelings hiding in it. It's abstract, but as my circle of friends helped me understand on our picture-perfect discussion night, though you might not be able to define it—you know it when you see it! By the end of this chapter, you'll hone in on your particular areas of insecurity and better understand the pitfalls of putting your trust, your worth, and your identity in things that can't be sustained.

My friend Fran—the one who had to move out of her dream house and into her mom's home—is the best kind of authority on insecurity because she's searingly honest *and* she's a hairstylist. Everyone who's had a relationship with a hairstylist knows what a special place he or she holds in a woman's heart. Give a woman the bangs she's dreamed of or the highlights that remind her of the beach and that woman is yours forever. So when Fran talks insecurity—what she's seen and heard—we should listen.

DEFINING THE ISSUE

Fran spoke first. "An insecure woman is someone who talks with no opinion. She can expend an enormous amount of energy to avoid uncovering anything about herself. If she does give an opinion, she tends to pull it back or second-guess what she just said. I think she's someone who will sometimes joke about herself in a painfully self-deprecating way. When I'm around a woman like that, I get the feeling that she doesn't know who she is, or she doesn't like what she knows about herself."

You probably don't fit Fran's description perfectly, but my guess is that you tend to cover certain areas in your life because of your own sense of "emptiness" or inadequacy. Insecurity is the recognition of an area of vulnerability, the general sense of dis-ease in one's own skin. Insecurity presents itself both as a trait of our personality, affecting every area of life, and as a circumstantial response when we are confronted with certain uncomfortable situations. In both cases, insecurity reveals those places where we feel exposed and inadequate. Insecurity can also tell others what aspects of ourselves we see as extraordinarily important: places where we might even set up idols, shrines to ourselves that we go to great measures to sustain and build.

It is almost laughable to ask *if* you struggle with insecurity because I believe we all do to a certain extent. So I invite you to take this assessment to discover *how, why,* and *where* you are prone to insecurity in your own life.[1]

INSECURITY ASSESSMENT

Take the following assessment to determine where insecurity arises in your life. Don't think too long before responding: just answer "mostly true" or "mostly false" for each of the following statements:

1. If I haven't heard from a friend in a while, I assume I've done something to offend her and she doesn't like me anymore.
   ____ mostly true   ____ mostly false

2. I am uncomfortable with my husband's/boyfriend's female coworkers/ friends.
   ____ mostly true   ____ mostly false

3. If someone compliments my appearance, I find myself unable to accept the compliment or I play it down. It's hard to just say thank you.
   ____ mostly true   ____ mostly false

4. I feel really stupid if I come to an event or meeting dressed down compared to everyone else.
   ____ mostly true   ____ mostly false

5. I don't like even my husband to see my body.
   ____ mostly true   ____ mostly false

6. When I receive feedback at work about how to do something better, I find myself really crushed.
   ____ mostly true   ____ mostly false

7. I have difficulty making decisions. Even after getting input from friends, family, or coworkers, I often second-guess my choice.
   ____ mostly true   ____ mostly false

8. I love knowing that others approve of my choices.
   ____ mostly true   ____ mostly false

9. When people speak abruptly or seem to be ignoring me, my first thought is I must have done something to offend them.
   ____ mostly true   ____ mostly false

10. I avoid those situations where I fear I might fail or appear not as capable as others.
    ____ mostly true   ____ mostly false

11. I think "Little Miss Critical" lives in my head and she has a lot to say whenever I fail to live up to my own standards.
    ____ mostly true   ____ mostly false

12. I sometimes do things for others that I don't really want to do because I'm worried about what they would think if I said no.
    ____ mostly true   ____ mostly false

INSECURITY: NOT JUST FOR MIDDLE SCHOOL

Late one evening, in the comfortable atmosphere created by semi-darkness and french fries from the drive-through, I sat in my SUV chatting with a few girls about how they were navigating life and faith in eighth grade.

"What's your biggest challenge?" I asked one of the girls between sips of Slushee, letting the question hang in the space between our burgers.

"Insecurity," she responded, quite confidently given her response.

"Insecurity about . . . ?" I quizzed.

"Everything. Looks. Friends. Boys. Grades. Family . . ." She trailed off as I marveled at how hard it is for women of all ages to figure out just who we are supposed to be.

Insecure is the catchphrase for just about every issue one can face as a woman. When mothers would bring their daughters to my office for counseling, insecurity was the reason behind their daughters' eating disorder or promiscuity or bullying. Insecurity was the reason their daughters hated their lives, the reason they made failing grades, the reason they quit the team. Insecurity explained my older teen clients' devastation over a breakup, anxiety about graduating, or lack of confidence to try out for the school play.

And although the reasons changed, insecurity remained a catchphrase for adult women in the counseling office as well. Insecurity was why they didn't ask for the raise. Why they didn't become vulnerable in a relationship. Why they shrank to the corners rather than stepping to the front. Insecurity—and the oppressive feelings that accompany it—partnered with just about every issue these women faced.

Insecurity is like mold in my kitchen: it's never welcome but it seems to crop up in all kinds of places. The difference is this:

I would never let mold remain on my bread or in my refrigerator, yet so often we women readily accept insecurity like it's a normal part of life. Friends, I do not believe that this is what God intended! This is not just an issue for self-help books or a therapy-happy generation. I believe our insecurities are fundamentally a spiritual issue. The unbalanced and unmoored feelings that accompany insecurity betray some truths about our heart that we must examine if we are to offer love and freedom to others.

THE SHAM OF WORLDLY SECURITY

Review your responses to the insecurity assessment. Are you uncomfortable? Do you wish some of them weren't true? Are you frustrated that some of the same issues you've had with appearance or approval since middle school continue to plague you today? Here's a disappointing reality of life: our emotions often defy our logic! We know all the right things to tell ourselves:

"This isn't about what other people think!"
"Just be yourself!"
"You are loved!"

And my personal favorite, "Find your security in Christ!" (more on that in chapter 6). But the reality is, believing these things is much harder than saying them. So hard, in fact, that these phrases, though true, become hollow platitudes that do nothing except make us feel worse!

I would not readily dub author and blogger Rachel Held Evans insecure. When we met over dinner before a writing conference, I marveled at her humility coupled with a genuine sense of ministry via her blog and book. And all this at age twenty-eight! Yet this same confident, intelligent woman who in my eyes had clearly "arrived" once blogged on her own journey: "My insecurities keep me from participating in meaningful relationships, doing things that are out of my comfort zone, and learning from new perspectives."[2] The shakiness of insecurity creates a desperate feeling in us to hide or cover ourselves from further exposure. This leads us to a paralysis within us. Rachel's assessment of the problems insecurity creates in her is the true tragedy of this issue. Without facing our issues head-on, we miss out on some of the richest gifts life offers, like growth, love, and adventure.

Let's dive in and examine the particular strain of your insecurity issue.

Appearance

If you answered "mostly true" to statements 3, 4, and 5, appearance may be a place of insecurity for you. You and I come by our obsession with appearance naturally. One of the first compliments you ever received probably had to do with physical beauty. Before you were even out of the hospital nursery, women were dressing you in pretty pinks and cooing over your perfect features.

Let's face it, babies don't do much . . . so we look at them and find something to say about their appearance. While our knees were still knobby and our cheeks still chubby, we were already attracted to attractiveness. Researchers have discovered that babies as young as two days old stare longer at faces judged attractive by adults.[3] Other research shows that this obsession with beauty permeates every aspect of life: people judged as attractive tend to do better in school, make more money, be found "not guilty" more often in court, and generally perform better in every kind of social situation. However, the exceedingly rigid stereotype of what we find beautiful means that basing our worth on our appearance leads to a maddening race where we always lose.

Insecurity's greatest victory is keeping you doing . . . nothing.

The average teen now sees more pictures of outstandingly beautiful women in one day than her mother did during her entire adolescence. Not only do we see more pictures of a higher standard to compare ourselves to—less than one percent of the female population has the height, weight, or facial features of top models—but we can't even evaluate ourselves objectively. Up to eight out of ten women are dissatisfied with their appearance when looking in a mirror, and many actually see a distorted image. And that image isn't even the same every day, according to the Social Issues Research Centre's findings on appearance: "Sex, age, ethnic group, sexual orientation, mood, eating disorders, what they've been watching on TV, what magazines they read, whether they're married or single, what kind of childhood they had, whether they take part in sports, what phase of the menstrual cycle they're in, whether they are pregnant, where they've been shopping—and even what they had for lunch"[4] all contribute to one's evaluation of whether their appearance is worth being happy about. Take an abnormal amount of emphasis on appearance and add a near-impossible standard, and you get the wild (yet perfectly made-up) eye of a woman who lives in the upheaval of an identity focused on appearance.

Relationships

If you answered "mostly true" to statements 1, 2, and 9, relationships may be a place of insecurity for you. One of my favorite new reality shows is the competition *So You Think You Can Dance*. The young competitors are talented and expressive, dazzling viewers with a combination of artistry and athleticism. In the televised portion of the competition, the male and female contestants are paired off and perform choreography from different genres of dance. The majority of the stories portrayed on stage are about love. Love lost. Love begun. Rocky relationships. Affairs, betrayal, lust, and temptation are played out, week after week. The height of our experience of life is found in love—at least according to this show and most pop culture.

Television, radio, the big screen—almost every story involves a love story. Often the stories told in church are no different. Proverbs 31 (which is clearly about a *married* woman) is touted as the ultimate ideal of womanhood. It's no wonder that so many of us look for our worth in relationships—and ultimately, "the one." We cling tightly to the belief that if only we were known, loved, cherished, and believed in by that special someone, all of our insecurities would disappear.

Lindsay is a great example of this principle. Lindsay and I became friends in our twenties. I was struggling through being a newlywed while she was struggling with being single. No matter what I said about finding security in Christ (and how marriage didn't make me secure), Lindsay was convinced that it would all be different if and when she was married. And when she finally did marry (closer to thirty than twenty) it *was* good. But it turns out, marriage didn't make Lindsay more secure. Having children and a husband is a wonderful thing—but it didn't solve Lindsay's insecurity problem. In fact, her first years of marriage were tumultuous because she discovered that her new husband wasn't equipped to be her "everything" and that he wasn't always the rock she had hoped for.

Lindsay and I both found out that looking for security in a relationship alone is an impossible task. In all of us, there is a part of our hearts that desperately seeks to be understood, supported, and delighted in; a part that wants someone to cheer us when we are discouraged, calm us when we are frustrated, soothe us when we are sad; and this part of our hearts can never be fully satisfied by one flawed human. I would love to have the perfect husband and the perfect circle of friends who somehow know me better than even I know myself. Yet when I examine my own heart, I realize I can't even meet my own standard. I can't give what my heart demands to receive.

When the friend, boyfriend, husband, or child doesn't meet the deep cravings in our souls, we tend to demand too much—or turn inward and create a fortress where we claim to need nothing. We are uneasy in our relationships because we don't even know what we should want or expect out of others.

We demand of our relationships with others that which even we ourselves cannot give.

This waffling between the sense that we deserve more from others and the fear that we are nothing special leaves us pitching back and forth wildly in our relationships and ultimately accomplishes insecurity's greatest coup: keeping us overly focused on ourselves. And there is nothing that keeps us from living in freedom like the soul vacuum of self-focus.

Approval

If you answered "mostly true" to statements 7, 8, and 12, you may place too much stock in others' approval. My friend Emily puts her desire for approval this way: "My insecurity actually goes up when I'm around people I admire. . . . I feel like I don't measure up when I'm around people whose opinion I care about. I feel really unstable and unsafe, so I don't trust myself or my actions. I get quiet and awkward, which only makes it worse."

In our desire for something that tells us we are "good enough," approval becomes our measuring stick. Who doesn't like to bask in the glow of another's affirmation? But there's a fine line between enjoying the approval of others and becoming an approval junkie—moving from experience to experience looking for your next affirmation "fix." At the heart of it, a craving for approval creates a constant striving in our souls. Because we measure our worth by the admiration of the person whose approval we crave, we seek to do more and more of whatever earns their favor. And as we do, we often stray further away from the "realness" of who we are.

My friend Kristy can weave together a joke and deliver it with perfect timing. But she also has a passionate heart for God and the ability to teach Scripture. Kristy sometimes struggles to find the balance between basking in the approval of those who love her for being a jokester and choosing to seek the deeper places of her own heart as she develops her ability to teach. Have you ever considered what personality traits others approve of in you and how you tend to "play" to those? Do you ever do it to the detriment of other aspects of your personality or gifting?

Achievement

If you answered "mostly true" to statements 6, 10, and 11, you may place much of your worth in what you can accomplish. Social scientists have discovered a trend among high-achieving women that they've dubbed "the imposter phenomenon." A study of 150 successful career women with advanced degrees indicates that many women, despite overwhelming evidence to the contrary, live with a deep-seated fear that they will be "found out" as phonies— posers who truly don't have the intelligence or achievement to be lauded in their industries. If you were considered intelligent as a child, you might relate. The study goes on to talk about women who were dubbed either the "social" child of the family or were considered "perfect" early on. The social ones constantly felt the need to prove their intelligence; the perfect ones struggled with a deep sense of inadequacy when they couldn't live up to the "indis-criminate praise" that their well-meaning parents lavished onto every aspect of their life.[5]

When I walked into my first college orientation session between my proud parents, I had no idea how the words spoken in that dark lecture hall would stick with me for years to come. One of the professors who welcomed us opened with these lines: "I've got news for you. You are all at the top of your high school class. You are all high achievers in academics and extracurriculars. You are all the cream of the crop. But here you are all just normal. The stage has been reset."

I didn't know how true those words were until I racked up a 2.5 GPA in my first semester and discovered that I actually had to work to achieve even a fraction of what I was used to experiencing in high school. It was only when my identity as a "good student" was stripped away that I realized just how important achievement was in making me feel strong and confident in all areas of my life. When my area of strength was challenged, it was as if my personal castle had been stormed—the door blown open to all kinds of insecurities I had held back by claiming my worth in achievement.

To this day, the temptation to place my worth in achievement plagues me. A high mark—in school, in life, in ministry—seduces me to believe this is the ultimate "definer" of me. It wasn't until I stayed home with my children that I realized how deeply connected my identity was with achievement. My achievement-oriented self wanted the fix for my problems to be something I could study up and get tested on, without ever having to live through it. But life doesn't operate like a multiple-choice test, and my own experiences with insecurity have been healed only through the uncomfortable exposure that comes when God leads us away from the things we hold close. When I stopped racking up high marks—when all I was left with was my yoga pants, Dansko clogs, a stroller, and a sinkful of dishes—I truly learned what it meant to be tangled in and then freed from insecurity.

ALL TANGLED UP

Have you ever been tangled in fishing line? The thin line is almost invisible, but its appearance belies its strength. Every move you make to free yourself only traps you more. It takes great patience and focus to hold still and untangle a fishing line, and the same is true of your insecurity.

The idea of insecurity paralysis relates to the word *snare* in Scripture. In Psalm 25, David describes this feeling as being trapped as if his foot were caught in a snare, much like a fishing line. The more one struggles, the tighter the snare becomes. But unlike fishing line, David explains how to get free in a much different way.

In Psalm 25:15, David writes, "My eyes are ever on the LORD, for only he will release my feet from the snare" (NIV).

It seems logical that we should examine our entanglement to find the root of our problem, to begin the painstaking process of freeing ourselves from the snare. It seems like insecurity should be something we can "think" our way out of by painstakingly picking apart every thin snare that holds us paralyzed. Yet Scripture points out that the only way to be truly released is by focusing our attention on God. In the next chapter, we'll look at the truths found in Scripture and how to keep our focus on them while God releases us from the snare of our insecurities.

Insecurity keeps us self-focused and ultimately paralyzed in our life and relationships.

In the midst of all this insecurity talk, we can easily conclude that the things we cling to (appearance, relationships, approval, achievement) are really not good at all. If I overvalue my beauty, I can easily turn my back on all things about being pretty in my quest to get free of insecurity. But the pendulum doesn't need to swing so wildly.

Our love of the beautiful, our deep desire for meaningful

relationships, our hopes that we will excel in our work, our desire for approval—these are God-created experiences and desires! It's often the priority we give these things in our hearts that leads to our disappointment, disillusionment, and deep insecurity.

So we seek ways to find peace, to move from a place of clinging desperately to worldly security to abiding in a sense of great security that comes from our heavenly Father. This process is a necessary stage in our faith, and we must be kind with ourselves during it. We do not come by our insecurities easily, and we do not move away from them quickly. The growth required to finally rest in security and peace deep inside ourselves takes work. And that process can be a bit—awkward.

THE NECESSARY AWKWARD STAGE

Yesterday my daughter rode her bike next to me as I ran. While we both clambered up a hill on the way back home, I looked over for a moment and observed her pedaling, pumping her legs, leaning forward on her handlebars, focused on her goal. From head to foot, Cameron is a perfectly scaled little six-year-old.

I found myself involuntarily smiling at her cuteness when I realized the inevitable: someday she'll be awkward. It probably won't be for a while, but there will come a day when we might be climbing this same hill together and she'll seem very different. Maybe her legs will grow faster than her torso, and she'll lope like a gorilla instead of skipping like a gazelle. Maybe her hands will get big or her hips will grow before the rest of her. Her face will change, too, as she develops from girl to woman. I know she'll end up beautiful. But she won't escape that awkward but necessary stage of growth.

We recognize the awkward stage as part of our physical growth, but I think we forget about how we develop in other areas of life . . . emotionally, spiritually, and relationally. And I believe that our insecurities speak to the growth that we are still experiencing in our quest to become healthy, mature women. Like having size ten feet on a five-foot-two frame, growth is awkward. We want to have it figured out as soon as we become adults, to step away from years of struggling with our bodies the minute we get married, to leave our quest for perfection back with our college diploma. But when we find ourselves shaken in these areas and realize just what a grip they have on our hearts, we are given the opportunity to learn to focus less on these aspects of ourselves and develop a God-centered view of our souls. When we reframe our insecurities as guideposts on the road to growth, we may still feel awkward about them, but we'll also recognize them as totally necessary steps toward true freedom in Christ.

Angela came to counseling because she was crying every day but didn't think she had anything to cry about. Her two daughters, the joy of her life, were thriving as energetic high schoolers. But her younger daughter was going through a tough breakup with her boyfriend, and Angela (not the daughter!) had become unhinged. Angela knew that her deep despair at her daughter's pain wasn't quite right. And as we discovered together, Angela's tears were about more than just the breakup. They were about loss—the perceived loss of her daughters who would be out of the house (and not needing Angela) sooner than she would ever want, and consequently, the loss of Angela's identity as their mother.

In my desire to help Angela see life beyond motherhood, I once asked her to tell me about herself. "What do you like to do?" I asked. I remember my voice was very matter-of-fact as I waited for her to rattle off a list of things she enjoyed. But instead, I got silence. We sat there awkwardly. Looking at each other. Finally Angela said in a bewildered tone, "I don't know what I like. I've given everything to raising my girls. I just always do what they need or want. I've watched their ice skating and field hockey. I've hosted their parties and made cupcakes. I've driven all over town. I've been friends with their friends' mothers. I guess I don't know what I like."

This was the awkward stage of Angela's growth. A long season of mothering, in which Angela placed the very core of her identity, had caused her to lose her way. And when that role waned, Angela was shaken by her deep insecurity.

As a mother myself, I know that this role is consuming, often demanding our all. Even as I write these words, my toddler, up two hours early, is demanding that I turn on his morning television show. How difficult it can be to not base our purpose and identity in whatever consumes our time and energy. Yet there is a core of us that isn't about motherhood or even womanhood. It's the part of our soul that is created to find rest in God alone. And that part remains restless until it finds the deep rest of security in Christ. Friends, it is good to recognize our lack of this peace! And it is often only in the recognition of our insecurity that we realize how we are longing for something more.

What if we began to think of our insecurities not as shameful places to hide but as opportunities to see God working in our lives? When we begin to understand how our insecurities work in our minds, we begin to see just where we need God's healing touch or transforming confrontation.

The journey of insecurity is a necessary process to discovering a Christ-centered identity.

Now in my head I'm imagining some of you sisters are talking right back to this page. "Nicole," you say, "I've been an approval junkie for decades! There's no changing me now. . . . I've tried but it's never worked before." So let me tell you what I learned from Angela. It turns out that Angela used to love to write. She had stuffed that love down in the busyness of motherhood, but in our time together, she began to write again. And as she did, she rediscovered some of herself. She created a space bar for her pen and journal. The writing uncovered pages of insecurities. But she also used those pages to rediscover her security in Christ, based on the promises in the next chapter. And as she found her security in Christ, she found herself again.

So if we were having this conversation face-to-face like Angela and I did for many hours, I'd probably grab your hand. Then I'd ask you if you believe that God can work miracles. Because no matter what your age, no matter how deep those insecurities run, no matter what the circumstances are that created these shaky places—God is able. He is a miracle worker. He specializes in situations that seem bleak, in people the world calls goners, and in cemetery places of the soul. He is a life giver in every sense of the world—and you are never outside of his grasp.

Every place of insecurity in your life; every situation where you find yourself paralyzed or shaky, every circumstance or season that makes you wonder if you are "good enough": these are the places where God does his best work. But getting centered on the rock of God's love takes some doing. The next chapter will examine the central promises of Scripture that support our search for security in Christ alone.

SPACE BAR

A PRAYER

My Father God, it's hard to remember that you not only love me, but that you like me—in all my insecurities, in the ways that I wander away from you, and even in the ways I consistently try to find life in things that can't satisfy. Jesus, would you cover me with your love, showing me today exactly how you love me? I want to trust you to satisfy me, especially in the places where I feel so insecure. Amen.

A JOURNALING EXERCISE

1. Complete this statement: If I didn't have _____
   [friendship, body shape, attractiveness, approval, etc.], I don't know
   who I'd be. If I were not a _____ [mother, wife,
   hard worker, etc.], I'd be lost.

2. Take some time to write about why these things are particularly
   important to you. Are there some people, roles, or circumstances that
   have more power over you than you'd like? Are there stories from
   your past or your family that relate to these insecurities? Remember,
   this is not an exercise in condemnation or shame. This is a way to
   face your own reality so that you can ask God to intervene and grow
   you beyond your insecurities.

   _____

   _____

   _____

   _____

   _____

FOR GROUP DISCUSSION

1. How would you define insecurity? What does it look like to you?

2. Think of your physically awkward stage. Were you insecure? What
   (if anything) has changed since then? Now consider what area of
   life feels "awkward" now. Is it your level of emotional maturity? Your
   ability to trust in God? Your struggle with approval addiction?

3. From whom do you desire approval? What would it be like if you
   were to lose that approval?

4. What are the if-onlys in your life? What do you imagine life would be like with those if-onlys in place?

5. Have you experienced insecurity paralysis? What has it kept you from experiencing?

Find out from Nicole how God can use your insecurity. Snap the code with your smartphone or visit the link below.

www.tyndal.es/ShesGotIssues5

CHAPTER 6

ATTACHING YOUR ANCHOR

Faith is a living, daring confidence in God's grace, so sure and
certain that a man could stake his life on it a thousand times.
MARTIN LUTHER

I ONCE HAD A CLIENT with a recurring dream about storms. The fright in her eyes and the way she recounted the dream to me brought it to life, even as we sat together in the safety of my office. In the dream, my client was caught in a large, deserted space during a vicious storm. As the winds kicked up and the rain began to fall, she searched frantically for protection. She built a shelter out of sticks and hid herself in it, hunkering down and curling up to keep safe. But the wind howled, ripping her shelter apart. The sticks whipped away from her, some hitting her as they disappeared. And she was left with no shelter at all, just her . . . and the storm.

This dream occurred several times over the months we saw each other. The dream increased in intensity. The storm in her dream would whip and wail until she would jolt awake, gripping her blankets and shaking.

But one day she came in and told me that the dream had changed. As in every earlier dream, she was left exposed and vulnerable, with nothing to cover and shield her from the enormous power of the storm. But this time, a man arrived. She saw his feet but was too scared to look up. Was he a villain—another man, who, just like the men in her past, meant her harm? Or could it be that this man who visited her dreams, who showed up in the storm—could it be that this man was different?

THE STORM OF INSECURITY

Throughout Scripture, storms are used to display God's power, both to those who oppose him (as in Exodus 9) and to those who fear him (as in Exodus 19). God sometimes speaks from the storm (Job 38:1) and sometimes in the whisper after the storm (1 Kings 19:12). Nahum 1:3 says, "He displays his power in the whirlwind and the storm." In a way that is uniquely God's, he can create, use, and shelter us from every storm we might face.

Our lives can reflect my client's dream. We are often caught, vulnerable and exposed, when life's storms come. The storm may rage outside of us—our parents' sudden divorce. The bitter taste of rejection. Wounds inflicted by others that have never healed. The storms may rage inside of us—a funnel cloud of emotions that seem to gather strength and spill out into all areas of life. And when those storms rage, we find ourselves looking for something—anything—to provide us shelter and protection. We pretty ourselves up and take any scraps of affection that come our way. We seek approval as the calm for our storm, hoping for even a brief respite when we will feel like all is well. We pour ourselves into work or competition. We build our own stick houses and declare them fit for living in, and they hold up—for a while.

But in God's fierce mercy, he rips those flimsy shelters away. He allows the wind to blow and to expose how fragile those shelters really are. Whatever we grip on to for security eventually blows away, sometimes wounding us in the process. In that terrifying moment we are exposed. The things we hide beneath for temporary shelter prove to be shams. This is the trial we will face—again and again—whenever we put our trust in anything outside of God.

If you've experienced the storm of insecurity, you know what it's like to cling to something that feels shaky. You know what it's like to put your hope in a shelter that keeps falling apart! But there is good news in this mess. The God who can bring the wind and rain can also provide refuge in the storm.

Hebrews 6:18 says that "we who have fled to him for refuge can take new courage, for we can hold on to his promise with confidence." Notice that God calls us to do just one thing: we must flee! *Flee what?* you may wonder. During our "awkward phase" of spiritual growth, which is often precipitated by a storm, we realize, perhaps for the first time, just how quick we are to put our security in our appearance, approval, performance, or achievement. Only when we realize what a shabby imitation these are for true shelter and security are we willing to seek real refuge. We must turn our backs and flee, letting go of what we held on to as our "identity" so that we may find true shelter.

This concept of fleeing—turning from one thing to pursue another—is like the concept of repentance that Jesus referred to when he invited his hearers into relationship with him. Even as he astounded them through his miraculous touch of healing, Jesus declared to all who would hear:

> The God who sends the wind and rain also provides refuge in the storm.

"Repent, for the kingdom of heaven is at hand!" (Matthew 3:2, NKJV). The Greek word for repent, *metanoeo*, implies the act of changing the condition of the mind. Repentance is turning;

metanoeo is changing. This kind of repentance is "fundamentally tied to the mind or heart and not the emotions."[1] This is good news for all of us who worry that our faith has to be something we "feel" at all times. The repentance mentioned in the gospel, the turning and fleeing from earthly security to a rest found only in God's promises, doesn't wait for our emotions.

We discipline ourselves in our minds to receive the truth of Christ's security. As those truths begin to sink deeply into our souls, as we fix our eyes on the Lord and flee to him, we find ourselves miraculously free of the tangles of insecurity. That's because when we run to Christ for security, we find a hope that is "a strong and trustworthy anchor for our souls" (Hebrews 6:19). This little phrase has become my mantra against insecurity. Everything in me wants to "think" my way out of insecurity. But I've found that the way out comes not by thinking harder about a particular problem but by focusing my energy upward to Christ: "Let us fix our eyes on Jesus, the author and perfecter of our faith" (Hebrews 12:2, NIV).

Right now, wherever you are and whatever your circumstances, whether your issues seem too small to bother God with or too immense even for him—you can begin to flee. Flee from your own way, turn from those comfortable but shaky places to which you fix your soul, and set your eyes clearly on the security you can find only in Christ.

WORD UP

In the swirl of Christian culture and nice-girl churchianity, we often lose the very essence of what Christ offers us in himself. That's unfortunate, because Scripture makes clear the soul-shaking benefits of inviting Christ to be the ruler of our hearts, whether we've been following Jesus for decades or are still unsure where we stand with him. These benefits are the building blocks of a secure heart. They create the foundation by which we live and the filter we use to alert us when we are tempted to find our worth in any other aspect of our identity.

Without understanding the benefits of our relationship with Jesus, we are fundamentally insecure. Our lives are built on shifty substitutes. When we discover places of insecurity, we must return to the fundamental promises of Christ. This truth can be one of those ideas that sound good on paper but are hard to translate into real life. I get that; I've struggled with it myself. But I believe that there is power in God's Word. Romans 12:2 says, "Let God transform you into a new person by changing the way you think."

If you've struggled with these truths, can I challenge you? Will you fix your mind on the promises of God for the next week? Every time you feel ashamed, unforgiven, or not worth God's love, repeat a verse you learn in this chapter (listed at the end). The first day, you might need to repeat one a dozen times! But the next day—or the next—you will find that something's changed. This is the power of the Holy Spirit, doing for us what we cannot do for ourselves. God's Word is a healer, a transformer, and a re-creator of our hearts and minds. We just have to do the work of getting that Word *in*.

Christ offers forgiveness from sin

At this point in your story you've probably figured out that you are not, in fact, good. Few of us make it very far into adulthood without realizing how messed up we really are. As Paul says in Romans 7:15, "I don't understand myself at all, for I really want to do what is right, but I don't do it. Instead, I do the very thing I hate." We want to do right but we don't. We start off with good desires, but somewhere along the path they get twisted, distorted. We find ourselves clinging to a flimsy shelter we've created for ourselves, lost in a storm with no foundation. This is the exact place where Christ enters in.

Jesus knows the exact condition of our heart, even when we cannot perceive it. Jeremiah 17:10 says, "I the LORD search the heart and examine the mind" (NIV). And it's during our storms that he offers to set our hearts straight—from our past, from our present, and even from our future sin. No other figure in history has offered this kind of complete reconciliation.

The prophet Isaiah foretold the work of Jesus: "By his knowledge my righteous servant will justify many, and he will bear their iniquities" (53:11, NIV). Not only did Jesus do an amazing work for us by sacrificing his life for ours, he did it willingly, by his own knowledge, because of his great love for us. Romans 5 says that God backed up his love for us with action, that Christ willingly bore our sin upon himself so that we might experience complete forgiveness. And with this forgiveness comes great freedom in the here and now.

Christ offers freedom from guilt

Galatians 5:1 declares, "It is for freedom that Christ has set us free" (NIV). Another way to say it is that when we accept the gift of Christ's work for us, our hearts are set free from the world's or our own self-imposed chains. We are free from the burden of our own inability to be right.

Christ has given us freedom, not just from sins of our past. Rather, this freedom offers the promise of a clean start every day and every moment of our lives. This freedom is about the opportunity to be in the presence of a holy, powerful, and loving God. The writer of Hebrews says we can "approach the throne of grace with confidence" (4:16, NIV). *Confidence.* We walk into the presence of our powerful, present God because he allows us to do so! We bring our requests before him with *confidence* because he designed it that way! Because Christ's work allows us access to God's presence, we are able to do all things through him. All things.

Whatever the world brings our way, whether sorrow, or trouble, or sin, or temptation, we can do it all "through Christ, who gives me strength"(Philippians 4:13).

Security in Christ creates the freedom to actually be changed, to be transformed into a woman who acts, feels, and thinks differently because of God in her life.

When we accept the gift of Christ's work for us, we are freed from the burden of our own inability to be right.

My counseling supervisor once told me that it's futile trying to change people by shaming them. We may change our outward behaviors because of cajoling, punishment, or shame—either the shame of others or our own voices of shame—but we are only truly transformed by love. It is when we flee from our own self-hate and surrender to God's love that any kind of change becomes possible.

Christ offers eternal life

Forgiveness of sin and freedom from shame accompany the promise of eternal life. "And this is the way to have eternal life—to know you, the only true God, and Jesus Christ, the one you sent to earth" (John 17:3). In our daily struggles and trials, eternal life can seem like a far-off platitude, not "real" enough to make a difference in our daily lives.

In a popular sermon, author Francis Chan used a long rope and a little red tape to illustrate eternity.[2] With the rope stretched from one end of the stage to the other, Chan told his congregation to imagine the rope going on forever, across the country and around the world several times. Then he held up the beginning of the rope, the first two inches wrapped in red tape. "You see this red part?" said Chan. "This would represent your time on earth." The visual image of an eternal timeline with a tiny portion marked for our earthly life sticks with me. Everything on earth—every joy, every pain, the mundane and the magnificent—is put in proper

SHE'S GOT ISSUES / NICOLE UNICE

perspective when considered in light of eternity. The reality of our true lifetime is as real as that rope held in Chan's hand. "Where, O death, is your sting?" asked Paul in 1 Corinthians 15:55 (NIV), reflecting on just how our perspective is changed by the security of life and death and beyond with Christ!

It is eternal life that gives us the perspective to bear all things on earth. We so easily become mired in our daily struggles unless we discipline our minds to remember that there is more than what we see here! My friend has a personal mantra: "heaven is better." When he finds himself struggling with an earthly desire, he whispers, "Heaven is better." When the going gets tough, he reminds himself and me that "heaven is better." This is a promise that gives perspective.

Christ offers a continual relationship with God

Ajith Fernando, the former national director of Youth for Christ in Sri Lanka, describes our relationship with God as the most basic difference between Christianity and every other religion. "[Grace through Christ] opens the door to a relationship with God that in turn opens the door to life's most fulfilling experiences."[3] It is almost beyond comprehension to believe that by merely accepting the grace of Christ and believing that we are freed by Christ's work, we have immediate and unlimited access to the Creator of the universe. It is an astonishing truth that should make our jaws drop in wonder. The same force that placed the stars in the sky, that forms a baby in a womb, that creates and calm storms—we can access that? that power? that grace? that great love? Yes, yes, and a resounding *yes*.

The fruit of our belief is an overwhelming sense of love and gratitude in God's presence. This is the discipline of our souls, to continually remind ourselves of the hope and security that come from Jesus' work in our lives.

Whenever insecurity pops up in your day—whether while you are feeling forgotten while loading the washing machine, overwhelmed at your desk, or misunderstood in a conversation, you can speak to yourself with a quiet reminder: *Jesus is with me. He gives me grace. He understands me in a way no one else can. I can be myself, free and flawed, because he loves me.*

Christ leaves the gift of the Holy Spirit

Not only does Christ perform the miraculous work of making us right yesterday, today, and tomorrow, but he gives his followers an amazing gift. "And when you believed in Christ, he identified you as his own by giving you the Holy Spirit, whom he promised long ago" (Ephesians 1:13). Scripture tells us that God's Spirit dwells within us the moment we believe. I'm not sure I can fully appreciate what it means to have the very Spirit of God dwelling within me. It certainly makes my trials seem less difficult.

A high schooler stopped in my office today to ask about my writing. As I shared with her the promises found in Scripture, her eyes glistened with tears. In that moment, I marveled about how deeply we are moved by the truth of God's promises for us and the freedom that comes from a relationship with Christ. To know that God knows each of us better than we know ourselves, that he holds all things together, and that he works all things together for good—these are the promises of our salvation. And these are the bricks that make up a sure foundation in Christ. Musician Mike Crawford wrote the song "Words to Build a Life On." The title alone describes our source of security, and the lyrics offer specific hope:

Blessed when you lose your own identity
Then blessed when you find it
And it has been redeemed[4]

These are the words we can build our lives on. We flee from and repent of our own shaky securities so that we can take hold of the hope that is the one sure thing of this world and beyond. My friend Becky put it this way:

> For me it's at an internal battle: where do I find my strength? If I am seeking approval/affirmation from others—I never make it very far. I constantly have to remind myself that I perform for an audience of one. Affirmation from this world is fleeting and superficial. Only Christ gives me strength and will allow me to feel secure with who I am, right now, no matter how I look, how smart I am, and how I perform in my work. Yet, I have to remind myself all the time, especially as someone who likes the check mark, the pat on the back, and the verbal affirmation.

Like choosing surrender over control, the choice to rest in Christ's promises rather than worldly sources of security must be made again every day. We will find ourselves seeking an anchor for our soul in all kinds of places, so we must return, repeatedly, to our sure foundation.

My client's dream of the wild storm, the faulty shelter, and the feet of a man didn't end with that scene. The last time she had the dream, she was in that same vulnerable place. But this time, after the sticks whipped away and she felt the full brunt of the storm, a calm came. The feet appeared again, and her terror increased as the man's hands reached down toward her. Then she felt those strong hands gently pull her up. In that moment she felt a deep

The choice to rest in Christ's promises rather than seek for worldly sources of security must be made again every day.

sense of peace and a compulsion to look at him, to look toward the only true thing that could calm the storm, create a refuge, and never let her go.

I believe Jesus invites every one of us to look deeply into his face as well. We fix our minds on our source of true security and anticipate that our feelings will, in fact, follow. And when we find ourselves clinging to the things of this world for strength, as we inevitably will, we can flee to him and return to our hope. He remains our secure anchor in the storm—the one thing, as Martin Luther says, worth staking our lives on a thousand times over.

THE PRACTICE OF TURNING

I have to admit that I feel a little insecure (ha, ha!) about leaving you with these truths alone. I do think each of us must find our own way to combat our unique brand of insecurity with the reality of God's promises. I asked several good friends this question: "When you feel insecure, what do you do to move back into a place of trust with God?" Most of them mentioned catching themselves in the act of "dwelling."

Melissa said, "I'm not much of a dweller, but when I find myself feeling insecure about a little thing, like what a fifteen-year-old thinks of my tennis coaching, a good strong self-talk usually works. I'm like, 'Melissa, snap out of it!' But when it's a big thing, I have to continually remind myself of God's promises and the fact that I want to trust him—that he's in control and that I can believe what he says."

Becky says it this way: "I find myself dwelling and I realize that I'm making a choice. I can choose to let a compliment about my hair be the thing I dwell on, or I can decide my butt looks bad in these jeans and I can think about it all day. But neither is a good choice. It's about deliberately choosing to turn my mind to other things, to fill myself with light and truth and not just flip through another magazine filled with supermodels."

Melissa and Becky have done the work of stepping outside of themselves to recognize when they are dwelling and deliberately turn (there's that word again) their minds toward the real truth about themselves.

SO WHAT IS SUCCESS?

Loving people takes energy. (Remember the symptom of compassion fatigue?) It takes confidence. And it takes security in Christ. So how do you know if you are becoming more secure?

A NEW SOURCE OF SECURITY

Here are a few things you can try when you realize you need to look again to Christ for your security:

1. Take a break from the fashion magazines, reality shows, and pop music. Consider adding some spiritual reading or worship music to your daily life instead. Try it every day for two weeks and see what happens!

2. When you find yourself dwelling on your insecurities, recite your ABCs. Starting with A, fix your mind on praising God from Scripture. It might go something like this. "A: God, you say you are Alpha and Omega, the Beginning and the End. B: Jesus, you are the Bread of Life. C: Thank you for giving us your Spirit as our Counselor. D: . . ."

3. Memorize a verse of Scripture to repeat in your mind whenever you need to "turn" your thoughts. Accentuate a different word with each recitation: IF anyone is in Christ, she is a new creation. . . . If ANYONE is in Christ, she is a new creation. . . . If anyone IS in Christ, she is a new creation. . . .

Secure women know their strengths and aren't afraid to own them. They also know about their weaknesses and aren't scared by them. Secure women can easily admit when they are wrong but don't beat themselves up about it. Secure women take risks. Secure women fail but try again. Secure women can be vulnerable with their friends. Secure women don't have to know all the answers. Secure women can say no. Secure women believe that love multiplies and that they can give lavish love and affection away because there will always be an abundance for them.

Truly secure women find their worth and their strength in Christ. They give up on the empty promise of worldly security, and in doing so, they find the deep love of true life (see Matthew 16:25) that Jesus offers. Secure women are beautiful, powerful women because of their deep ability to love—not because they do it perfectly, but because they are loved by a perfect God, who will "equip you with all you need for doing his will" (Hebrews 13:21).

SPACE BAR

A PRAYER

God, you have equipped me with a mind to learn your promises. I commit myself to you, to soak in the truth of your Word so that my heart might follow. I want to walk in the freedom of your truth and see the fruit of my security in you. Thank you for the promises of Scripture and the truth of the words that it's for freedom you've set me free. I pray that today I would live in that freedom in my mind, my heart, and my actions. Amen.

A JOURNALING EXERCISE

Look at the Scriptures listed below. What verse resonates with your life right now? Write it (or another verse you choose) five times in your journal. You may want to also jot it down on a note card and hang it on your mirror or tape it to your dashboard. Start with one truth you'd like to make your own this week, and do the work of writing it onto your soul through memorization.

> We who have fled to him for refuge can take new courage, for we can hold on to his promise with confidence. (Hebrews 6:18)

> Therefore, since we have been made right in God's sight by faith, we have peace with God because of what Jesus Christ our Lord has done for us. (Romans 5:1)

> Let us come boldly to the throne of our gracious God. There we will receive his mercy, and we will find grace to help us when we need it most. (Hebrews 4:16)

> I can do everything through Christ, who gives me strength. (Philippians 4:13)

> This is the way to have eternal life—to know you, the only true God, and Jesus Christ, the one you sent to earth. (John 17:3)

> No matter how many promises God has made, they are "Yes" in Christ. (2 Corinthians 1:20, NIV)

> When you believed in Christ, he identified you as his own by giving you the Holy Spirit, whom he promised long ago. (Ephesians 1:13)

> What this means is that those who become Christians become new persons. They are not the same anymore, for the old life is gone. A new life has begun! (2 Corinthians 5:17)

FOR GROUP DISCUSSION

1. Think about the storms that you've experienced in your life. How have they contributed to any particular insecurities?

2. Consider the five promises of security in Christ: forgiveness of sin, freedom from guilt, eternal life, continual relationship with God, and the gift of his Spirit. Which one is the most real to you? Which one is a challenge to accept? Why do you think that is?

3. Have you found a promise in Scripture that speaks specifically to an insecurity you experience? What is it?

4. What does a secure woman in Christ look like? What would it look like in your life tomorrow? How would you be different?

Nicole reflects on the five promises of security in Christ. Snap the code with your smartphone or visit the link below.

www.tyndal.es/ShesGotIssues6

CHAPTER 7

THE COMPARISON GAME

She wears high heels, I wear sneakers.
She's cheer captain and I'm on the bleachers.
TAYLOR SWIFT

I'VE HAD A LOVE/HATE RELATIONSHIP with comparisons for most of my life. I think it started with my first report card, but it cemented into my heart with my first set of standardized tests. Gripping my number two pencil tightly, I filled in a bubble sheet for the first time as a seventh grader. And when that printout came back to my desk, my name typed across the top and my scores listed down the side, I embraced this measuring stick of my worth with arms-wide-open abandon. With standardized tests, I didn't get ranked just with my class or even the other seventh graders in my state, but I was given a national average—*national*. And with that, my twelve-year-old heart found a place to camp out, a place to understand the world and myself as good, better, or best. When that sheet landed on my graffiti-scarred desktop, I found my way to feel "special."

SHE'S GOT ISSUES / NICOLE UNICE

By my sophomore year in college, my identity via comparisons had expanded well beyond grades and now included hip size. I would sit on one of the benches that flanked the dining hall entrance, and as female students passed by, I would compare my size to theirs. *Bigger, bigger, bigger, smaller. Smaller . . . bigger, bigger, same size? Bigger, smaller.*

From my vantage point on the bench, I was eye-level with hips. I was a hip-comparison expert. I watched hips in shorts, hips in dresses, hips in tight jeans, hips in pajama pants. I sized up every kind of thigh/butt/hip combination there was against my own mental self-portrait. Somehow, hip comparisons equaled how I should feel about myself. The hip game—and all the other ways I compared—became the barometer of my feelings.

Depending on how those feelings and the hip parade would collide, I could decide exactly how much to eat. I would sit at my table in the commons, talking boys, grades, and parties with my roommates or sorority sisters. All the while, I was a closet scientist, observing my friends' portion sizes and food choices, calculating calorie counts and metabolism rates and asking them if they wanted to work out that day.

I had one friend who ate without shame. Whenever I had lunch with her, I felt free to eat a bit more than usual. Because after all, my more was still less than her normal. And less, in my warped comparison mind, meant I was better, that I was okay. It meant that at least for a few hours between meals, I could deaden the cry of my soul, the part that wanted me to admit that I might not stack up so well against others after all.

Years later, I sat across my counseling office from Audrey, sent to see me by her parents because they didn't know what else to do, and sometimes mothers need reassurance when their daughters stop talking to them.

One day I asked Audrey if she thought she was attractive. "Um,

I don't know," said Audrey, staring at a blank spot on the wall, wrapping and unwrapping a long lock of hair around her finger. "It kind of depends."

Something about her way seemed familiar, and I took a deep breath before asking, "Do you ever play games trying to figure out if you are the prettiest one in the room?"

Audrey's bright eyes snapped to my face. She flung her long legs out from under her and leaned forward, "How did you know that?"

Over the next hour, Audrey detailed the elaborate ways she played the comparison game. She told me about watching other girls while she was running, contrasting their speed, outfit, and sweat output against her own. She explained that when she was at a party, she decided how she would feel after she gave herself a "ranking" based on other girls there. Comparisons determined Audrey's decisions about friendships, about boyfriends, about happiness, and about her body. Comparisons ruled her emotions, her self-worth, and her very life.

You may not struggle with comparisons like me or Audrey, but it's hard to escape the temptation to compare in our media-saturated, instant-access, celebrity-obsessed culture. So where do you stand with comparisons?

COMPARISONS ASSESSMENT

The purpose of this assessment is to get you thinking about the role of comparisons in your own life and relationships. Later in the chapter, we'll talk about three aspects of the comparison trap and how you can identify your issues with the help of this quiz. Put a check before each item that describes you:

_____ 1. I often measure myself against other people.

_____ 2. I sometimes determine my own worth/validation with thoughts like, *I'm as good as . . .* or *At least it's not as bad as . . .* or *I'm better than . . .*

_____ 3. It seems like life goes better/is easier for many people around me.

_____ 4. When a friend succeeds in an area that I excel in, I often find myself envious or resentful.

_____ 5. When I feel "on top of my game," everything feels right in the world.

_____ 6. I often worry that I don't measure up.

_____ 7. I keep a mental ledger in some relationships so I can track what I've done for someone versus what he or she has done for me.

_____ 8. The reality that "life isn't fair" frequently bothers me.

_____ 9. If I don't get my due, I find myself angry or anxious.

_____ 10. I struggle with "the grass is always greener" mentality.

WHY WE COMPARE

Comparing ourselves to others starts as a perfectly healthy stage of development. As children and into our adulthood, watching and imitating is the way we figure out how to do things like kick a soccer ball or make a new friend. Psychologist Albert Bandura called this social learning theory.[1]

This theory says that we look to those around us to determine our own way of thinking, feeling, and acting. As children, we look to our families. As teens, we start to look to our peer groups. As adults, what do we do? The same. One example of this is "keeping up with the Joneses," or in my case, "keeping up with the college gal's hip size."

Good things can come from observing others, such as aspiring to be like your mentor or becoming a writer after a positive experience with your high school journalism teacher (thanks, Mrs. Learmann). But sometimes I wonder if our ultracompetitive society encourages us to form an identity based solely on comparisons to those around us.

The competition that arises from comparisons segregates people based on their strengths, weaknesses, and personality. There are winners and losers, all-stars and benchwarmers, "us" and "them." Competition and comparisons also separate us in our relationships. Every friendship seems to have its own ledger. Our inter-

Comparison is healthy when it challenges me to be a better person; it's toxic when it tells me who I am as a person.

actions with others help us decide how we feel about ourselves. Rather than offering our unique selves to each other in love, we spend an enormous amount of energy evaluating our lives as if we had a divine measuring stick.

This measuring stick tells me how to feel about "me." Comparisons become an escape, a way to avoid embracing the reality of our lives and of ourselves—just as they are. Comparisons give us a reason to be happy or to be sad without paying too much attention to what's really going on. We think, *I feel sad today, but if I [cooked like Carrie, dressed like Dori, had money like Michelle, had a job like Jessica], then my life would be amazing.*

BLAME BOMBS

In the book of Genesis we find proof that the issue of comparisons is as old as the earliest relationships. Cain and Abel, the first children of Adam and Eve, illustrate in tragic detail what happens when the bitterness and jealousy of comparing come between brothers.

We catch up with Cain and Abel out doing their thing: Cain working the fields and Abel tending the flocks. Genesis tells us that each of the two brought an offering to the Lord. This offering was a way to thank God by presenting him with the work of their hands.

Genesis 4:3 (NIV) says that Cain "brought some of the fruits of the soil" as an offering. Compare this to Abel's offering, "fat portions from some of the firstborn of his flock" (verse 4, NIV). The passage goes on to say that God was pleased with Abel's offering but "he did not look with favor" (verse 5, NIV) upon Cain's. Uh-oh. Cain reacts to God's displeasure with unbridled rage. Next thing we know, Cain has killed his brother and been banished from his fields.

The likely problem was a heart issue embedded in the little details of the story. Cain brought "some" of his harvest while Abel brought the best of the firstborn lambs. This is the equivalent of Cain twirling a quarter in a vending machine for a plastic necklace made in Taiwan and Abel spending hard-earned cash on a beautiful gem. It's like Cain pulling up a beet on his way to the altar and Abel sacrificing one of the precious lambs he had tenderly cared for its entire life.

It was a heart issue. It was a motivation issue. And it was certainly an issue between each of the brothers and God.

When God called Cain out for his lack of gratitude and his halfhearted expression of worship, Cain responded by killing his brother. A little gap in reasoning, don't you think? I wonder if Cain thought to himself, *It's Abel's fault. If my brother hadn't been all goody-goody with his offering, then mine would have been just fine.* Cain thought God rejected his gift because he'd compared the two offerings. God actually dismissed Cain's crops because of Cain's heart.

Here's the deal: God doesn't grade on a curve. He knows you. He knows what you are capable of, what glorious love you can give, because he is your Maker. He isn't lining me up with everyone else and saying, "Oh, that Nicole—compared to other stay-at-home moms she's really not measuring up." Instead, he looks right into my own heart and says, "I know you, I know when you are giving me the real deal and when you are putting up a smoke screen. Do you recall all that stuff about knitting you together in your mother's womb? Yep. All true. Let's get real, and don't worry about anyone else."

Rather than looking at his own heart, Cain chose to compare himself to his brother. And that comparison and his subsequent actions ruined every important relationship in his life. Abel? Dead. Mom and Dad? Estranged. And God? God removed Cain from his presence, and Cain's rebellion against God continued with his stubborn refusal to accept the truth about that original offering. Abel didn't have anything to do with Cain's issues. Cain just did some blame bombing, and Abel was the unfortunate victim.

COMPARISON COMPLICATIONS

Now that we've seen how comparisons develop and what that looks like in Scripture, let's make it personal. Look back at the assessment earlier in this chapter.

If you put a check by a number of the statements, you may find yourself relating to one or more of the problems caused by comparisons. Even if many of the statements don't describe you, they might help you better understand someone in your life who is caught up in the comparison trap.

Problem #1: Looking at a parade through a peephole

If you checked items 1, 2, 9, and 10, pay attention to this couple's story: Tommy and Meghan are a typical couple, married nine years and raising two young girls. They live in the suburbs and both work full-time. If you walk by their home on a Saturday morning, Tommy might raise a hand off his lawnmower and wave energetically, and Meghan might chat with you while loading her little ones in the car for soccer. If you were the comparing type, you might even envy their life.

But when Tommy struggles at work and gets passed over again

for a raise, he looks around at his friends and can't help noticing how happy they all seem with their employers. They get bonuses and raises and always work fewer hours than he does. When Meghan plays tennis with her girlfriends, she can't help but notice that they get to play on weekday mornings while she slaves away behind a computer. Her friendships seem warm and close, but she's always on the outskirts, wondering why she can't have as easy a friendship with someone in the group as they seem to have with one another. When Tommy and Meghan find time to go out together, their conversation often turns to whining their if-onlys, and pining away about the friends and coworkers whose lives look easier and who seem happier.

Gals, this is a rookie mistake. Watch out for the deception of another's "better" life. Pay attention to the people around you long enough, and chances are, someone's happy marriage will disintegrate before your eyes. You'll discover your coworker's husband is an alcoholic. You'll find out that friendly woman you pass in the church nursery was so depressed last year that she didn't get out of bed for a month. Pain does not discriminate. Life happens. Jesus told his disciples "in this world you will have trouble" (John 16:33, NIV). He meant that each of us, in our own measure, will face pain. No one's life is immune, no matter how pretty the picture on the outside.

The distraction of others' seemingly perfect lives keeps us from enjoying our own.

I once counseled two girls from the same elite high school. These girls inhabited opposite sides of the popularity scale. Amanda was an artsy theater geek struggling with depression. Natalie was the all-American teenager, with the face and fashion to back it up—and she was also struggling with depression. Unless a girl has decided her identity is "troubled teen," being discovered at a counseling office feels like an embarrassing moment worthy of a

Seventeen magazine write-up. One day, despite my careful scheduling, Natalie flounced out of my office just as Amanda showed up. The space between the waiting room and my office door is about the size of a dot on a Twister mat, and at the moment we might as well have been three awkward preteens mixed up between "left foot red" and "right hand yellow."

Amanda's face went blank. She gripped her backpack and quickly fixed her gaze at the floor, paralyzed. Should she say hello? Ignore Natalie? Run screaming for the door?

Thankfully, popular Natalie saved the day. She put her hand on Amanda's shoulder and gave it a squeeze. "Hey!" she said brightly. "You come here? That is so cool! It's good to see you." Then she gracefully walked down the hall. Natalie's show of maturity and grace still makes my heart swell when I think about it. I was so proud of her in that moment.

For Amanda, that chance encounter may have been more healing than weeks of counseling. She was so stunned that Natalie punctuated her shopping trips to Saks and endless dates with football players with . . . counseling?

Amanda and I spent our whole session discussing that moment. We talked about the truth of real, messy life: that although we might look good on the outside, everyone has her own struggles to face. Looking into someone else's life from the outside and deeming it "better" is like looking at a parade through a tiny knothole,[2] an analogy William Young uses in the *The Shack* to describe our view of God's plan. We stare through that knothole, thinking we are seeing the whole picture, when in reality we see just a tiny glimpse of another person's reality.

Problem #2: Emotional tornadoes

If you checked items 3, 4, and 5 in the assessment, take note: giving yourself over to comparisons can lead to emotional turmoil.

And it's not always because of criticism, as my family's recent trip to the dentist illustrates. At our last all-family teeth cleaning, Dr. Rose, ultimate judge of teeth cleanliness, dubbed our clan as having "the cleanest teeth of any family I've seen." Hey, those of you who are also Dr. Rose's patients, sorry to break the news. Start flossing already.

What's amazing to me is that the offhand comment by Dr. Rose last Wednesday actually makes me feel good about myself! Inside I'm thinking: *Wow! Compared to other families, our teeth are clean! What a good mom I am. My kids are lucky to have me! Check out my glistening teeth! All is right in the world!*

This morning my daughter bounced up to me with peanut butter from her breakfast still on her lips. "Hon, go brush your teeth," I told her, a request that seemed to surprise her even though we do it every morning. As she skipped out of the room, I decided to time her. It took sixteen seconds for her to run upstairs to "brush her teeth" and return to my side. I don't even think the faucet went on, and the peanut butter was still smeared on her lip.

Somehow I don't think that's the kind of brushing the dentist had in mind, yet I still take pride in the dentist's comment . . . which has nothing to do with our family's actual hygiene. Yet I take that scrap of praise and bask in the glory. I let it inflate my own self-worth because I'm taking our dentist's words and using them as my own measuring stick of "good."

Here's the problem: if you let yourself be overly inflated by compliments, it won't be long before your bubble bursts. According to my friend Ashley, I am not a great cook. Even though Ashley's comments are not mean-spirited (and are, in fact, true), they can provoke me like a scratch I can't itch. They tickle my spirit, constantly bugging me, poking me, taunting me to have a conversation with them:

Ashley thinks you can't cook. Really, compared to your friends you aren't very competent. I mean, you graduated from college and you can't cook chicken? What kind of mom are you anyway? And, by the way, what's with Ashley? Did you eat her lasagna? It tasted like she plopped it out of a can and heated it with Sterno. Seriously.

But here's where comparisons are deceptive. If I let a little comment from Dr. Rose make me feel so good about my life, I also allow negative comments to make me feel crappy about my life. We don't preen and glow under compliments and remain unfazed by criticism. Anthony de Mello says it like this:

> If you get caught up in the judgments of people around you, you are eating the fruit of tension and insecurity and anxiety, because when today they call you beautiful and you are elated, tomorrow they will call you ugly and you will be depressed.[3]

Problem #3: Wasting energy trying to make life fair

If you checked statements 6, 7, and 8 in the assessment, consider how often lately you've thought, *It's not fair.*

Those are three words that I would love to strike from the English language. When God made my children, he cranked their internal-justice valves to the sheriff-of-the-world setting and then broke off the handle. The minutiae that they examine in their quest for justice is remarkable. Forget the cleanest teeth award. Our family should sign a Fair and Equitable Candy Disbursement Act into law. And woe to the adult who doesn't read the bylaws of this agreement. My pint-sized sheriffs will let you know about it, protesting in all manner of force, *"It's not fair!"*

But maybe my kids are like all of us, just more honest. There's nothing like candy to bring out the internal sheriff in everyone. I learned this vivid lesson when I sat in on a Sunday school class for tweens and their parents. Candy and Jesus were the theme of this class—heavy on the candy.

The kids came into class to find a lunch-sized paper bag plopped on each of their desks with their name on it—and their favorite candy inside. The students looked in their bags but were instructed to keep the contents a secret. I wish I could project a video of the experience into these pages . . . the looks on the kids' faces were unparalleled. The joy, excitement, and candy-before-10-a.m. mischievousness!

"Okay, kids, get in a circle," instructed the teacher. "How do you feel when you look into your bag?"

The kids shrieked with excitement, "Happppyyyyy!!!"

The teacher went on, "Now that we are sitting in a circle, I want you to take your paper bag and dump it out in front of you so we can all see what everyone has."

Whoosh. Once the candy was out of the bags, the joy rushed out of the room in an instant. Some faces went from smiling to frowning in protest, while others went from pleasant to guilty. Every bag had candy—but the amounts ranged from one minibar for some kids to a king-sized megabar of goodness for others. Every child had his or her favorite candy, but when they saw the quantities others had, they freaked out. They forgot their joy in the uproar of "That's not fair!"

There's nothing like comparison to keep us distracted from our own gifts. It worked both ways in that circle Sunday morning. The kids with a lot felt bad for their abundance. The kids with a little felt bad for their scarcity. And everyone became obsessed with fairness.

It's not totally our fault that we've got an internal justice meter. Lawrence Kohlberg, a developmental psychologist whose theory of moral development continues to influence psychology today, presupposed that all morality develops from our interest in justice.[4]

So when my kids say, "It's not fair," they are flexing moral muscles, trying to make sense of the world. And it makes sense that we would pursue justice since God made us in his image.

There's nothing like comparison to take away our joy in our own gifts.

Scripture tells us that God is just in all he does. The Bible uses the word *justice* when it commands that we "give each their due."[5] Deuteronomy 32:4 says that all of God's ways "are just; a God of faithfulness and without injustice, righteous and upright is He" (NASB). But as we discussed in the control chapter, God's ways are certainly not like ours. The apostle Paul said, "Now we see things imperfectly as in a poor mirror" (1 Corinthians 13:12). Yet we insist on evaluating our lives through that foggy mirror (and our tiny peephole). We don't trust an invisible God and his mysterious ways, so we choose instead to judge our own lives based on our partial picture of the true reality of life.

God is just. He has his way. But it's not our way. When we don't trust him, when the mirror is dull and the peephole is small, we often resort to our own way—using comparisons as a means to judge our lives. We figure that our idea of justice is *the* idea of justice. Problem is, our own distorted perception of ourselves leaves us wondering if God has given us the fun-size candy bar while endowing others with mega-king-size blessings. I'm beginning to understand that this way of perceiving reality withers my soul. As I've played the comparison game, I've found that I always lose because comparisons are what keep me from fully knowing myself and being fully available to know the ones I'm in relationship with.

In our quest to love others better, we must acknowledge and wrestle with our tendency to compare. Security isn't found in calorie counts or standardized test scores. I am sad for Audrey and the girls like her who base their self-worth on the size of their jeans and the prominence of their hip bones. But I have hope when I think of how God has enabled me to move beyond comparisons into a glorious, wide-open space where I feel the freedom to love what he's uniquely made in me. And in that freedom I've found the ability to also love what he's uniquely made in you. By closing the door on comparison, you, too, will open yourself up to an expansive love that's beyond measure.

SPACE BAR

A PRAYER

Father God, being free of comparisons sounds so great! My mind gets it, but my heart has a hard time following through. Once again, I'm at a place where I need you to intervene in my issues. Will you give me the ability to see myself as you see me, rather than comparing myself to others? I want to be free to love everyone with the gracious freedom you alone can give me. Thanks, God. . . . Amen.

A JOURNALING EXERCISE

Take a journey back in time. Who's the last person you compared yourself to? Take a moment to listen to your own thoughts about that experience. What were you accomplishing in that comparison? Did it make you feel better or worse about yourself?

_____

_____

_____

_____

_____

_____

FOR GROUP DISCUSSION

1. Do you agree that comparisons create a distraction from seeing your own inadequacies? How has that played out in your life?

2. Do you currently struggle with comparisons? If so, in what areas are you particularly tempted to compare yourself? If not, how did you move beyond the comparison game?

3. When it comes to justice, how do you try to take matters into your own hands?

Nicole offers a new perspective on a phrase we all use: "It's not fair." Snap the code with your smartphone or visit the link below.

www.tyndal.es/ShesGotIssues7

CHAPTER 8

QUITTING THE COMPARISON GAME

Most folks are about as happy as they make up their minds to be.
ABRAHAM LINCOLN

On a windy day in late March, my family trekked up I-95 to Washington, DC, for an afternoon of museum going, whining, and bickering. I wasn't planning on the whining and bickering, but that's as important for family bonding as the dinosaur exhibit in the Smithsonian.

As we headed into the Museum of Natural History, we fell in line behind a pack of six girls. Identical size, identical labels. Matching North Face jackets on top, designer skinny jeans on the bottom, finished off with furry Uggs.

I expect this conformed look out of young high school students. They are in the throes of adolescence, the "Sturm und Drang" (storm and stress), as psychologist Erik Erikson phrased the turbulent period of identity wrestling and hormonal pinball. But that picture of a six-pack of teenagers burned into my brain. They were so alike, from their straight-ironed hair to their L. L. Bean backpacks, yet I knew that each of them was created uniquely and gifted differently. Each had her own hopes and fears, her insecurities and sensitivities. But from the outside? You'd never know.

Not long ago I attended a neighborhood party for the grown-ups to celebrate the end of school. If time machines existed, I would swear those six teen girls in DC stepped into one and emerged as stay-at-home tennis moms at this party. No more skinny regular denim; these women wore skinny *white* denim. And silk tops. And open-toe, high-heeled sandals. I counted at least a dozen women in this attire before it was obvious I was staring.

I leaned over to my husband and said, "Do you see what I see?"

He answered, "Implants?"

That's a topic for another book, and after I punched him and pointed out the white jeans epidemic, he got it.

Maybe I'm overhyping the fashion trends, but the unspoken dress code exposed the enormous amount of energy we spend comparing our looks, our choices, and our ways to those around us. Some of that is normal, but if you've resonated with the red flag of using comparisons to determine your identity, then it's worth making some changes. Ever felt like this?

I want to be special but fit in.

I want people to recognize I'm unique, but consider me just one of the girls.

I am my own woman, but I want everyone to like me.

In a decade of youth ministry and counseling, I've heard thirteen-year-old teens and thirty-three-year-old women repeat these statements. Seems like we all want an identity based in both universal specialness and universal likability. If fashion trends formed the basis of my comparison study, then the style du jour requires us to sacrifice uniqueness at the altar of conformity.

So what does all this comparing do? At the core, comparisons turn our focus on ourselves. That self-focus blinds us to the needs of those around us. We become wholly incapable of the radical "love your neighbor" action that Jesus commands. And this is why comparisons are a major hindrance to a loving life with Christ.

CHANGE IN STATUS

In the last chapter, you identified your specific problem areas with comparison. Now let's move forward to understand how you and I can change our status:

Step # 1: Find your blind spots

There's no greater distraction from dealing with your own issues than filling your mind with comparisons. If you keep yourself busy evaluating your life against everyone else's (the peephole-at-the-parade problem), you can conveniently ignore the real problems of your heart. Like why you're discontent with where God has you. Like how to maximize your stage of life (single, married, divorced, etc.). Like sin, in general.

Psalm 146:8 says, "The LORD gives sight to the blind" (NIV). You and I need God to give us clear sight about our stuff. And we have to be willing to look at it head-on. This is a crucial step in identifying areas where we are prone to comparison—and I'm convinced we all have them somewhere. You can do this by being mindful of your internal dialogue—the running conversations you have with yourself. Some places you might be prone to compare yourself with others include:

Comparisons lead us to become ultrafocused on ourselves while also losing sight of who we really are.

- appearance
- relationships (dating, marriage, friendships)

- support systems (family, friends, church)
- work/career choices
- money
- spiritual life
- intelligence
- social aptitude

Allow me again to lay bare my own issues with an example. When Dave and I had our first son, we were overjoyed and underskilled. When we had our daughter less than two years later, we were overjoyed and overwhelmed and still underskilled.

All that overwhelmedness was due, in part, to my graduate school schedule and the fact that we didn't have any extended family in town. Now, my mom readers are thinking one of two things: *Extended family? Who has extended family in town? Where do you live, Mayberry?* or *Extended family? I have so much family in this town I can't get away from them if I tried.*

I am part of the first kind of family but live in a town full of the second type. I didn't know what it meant to have roots until I met my two best mom friends. Carrie lives three doors down from her mother. Beth's family *and* in-laws live within three square miles of one another.

That's a whole lot of babysitters and family parties and babysitters and Christmas dinners and babysitters and . . . that's just a bunch of people to cuddle and love on little children. Or at least that's the partial view I had of it compared to my own life! Anytime I felt overwhelmed by the financial strain of babysitters, or pined for a night away with Dave, or schlepped my two kids to my midwife appointment (now *that* is fun), my comparing heart told me how much easier life would be if only I had family around. These whisperings of discontent accomplished two things:

I disliked my family situation.

I disliked my friends for their seemingly better family situations.

The constant comparing led to resentment that took root as bitterness, a pervasive toxin that stole my joy.

That resentment stayed for longer than I would like to admit. I resented my extended family for not doing more. I resented my friends for what they could do that Dave and I couldn't. And like a contagious disease, this resentment spread even to my children. I loved them dearly but just wished there was more love for them somewhere else. Somewhere, preferably, where they could spend the night and I could sleep in.

I became the needy friend no one really wants to hang out with. A complainer. A joy sucker. In the infamous words of Pink, I was a hazard to myself:

It's bad when you annoy yourself,
So irritating.
I don't want to be my friend no more,
I want to be somebody else.

And I did want to be somebody else, somebody who wasn't incessantly comparing her own situation with others. No amount of resentment or complaining was going to change my situation, and I just got tired of it. I finally opened my eyes. I wanted the Lord to give sight to my blind spots. And did he ever!

The questions in the sidebar on page 132 helped me see my issues clearly.

Step #2: Open your heart

Step #1 was about asking God to show you your blind spots. Step #2 requires opening your heart. Earlier I quoted from Psalm 146:8,

COMPARISON: NOTE TO SELF

When you compare, ask yourself:

1. Why do I think this person's life is better/happier than mine?

2. What does she have, specifically, that I think makes it that way?

3. If I had that quality, how do I think my life might be different?

4. If the quality is attainable, what am I doing to make a change toward acquiring it for myself?

5. If the quality isn't attainable, how will I mourn what isn't and make peace with what is? How will I invite God to open my eyes to the blessings in my own situation?

"The LORD gives sight to the blind" (NIV). That verse continues, "The LORD lifts up those who are bowed down."

Remember our Bible buddy Cain? His blame game helped him ignore his own reality (sin) while resenting another (blame). His actual problem centered on his own inadequacy, disobedience, and stubbornness before God. The prophet Micah talks about what God really wants from us when we bow before him. He says we can bring our offerings, sacrifices, and good works, but what God desires is our humble heart (see Micah 6:8). It is when we come to him with hearts that are transparent and humble that he can lift us back up. It is in this exposed and vulnerable place that we are open to God's healing touch.

Once I discovered how comparisons were affecting my happiness and souring my relationships, I began to pay attention to my emotional responses. When I noticed myself comparing my situation to someone else's, I found resentment and disappointment were my go-to emotions. Over time, God began to show me how I used resentment to deflect painful feelings like sadness, rejection, and loss. When I looked deeper still, I found that my own selfishness and self-driven agenda were revving up my drive to compare.

I asked a friend of mine what he does when comparisons leave him feeling insecure and sorry for himself. He told me, "I have to humble myself before God. When I come to him in that place, he is always gracious to provide me with something—a person or a word or an experience—that encourages me to keep being exactly who I am, to be okay with how he's made me."

In the case of my extended-family dilemma, following these steps revealed how erroneous my thinking had become. When I opened my eyes, I saw how the family relationships of my best friends brought their own set of challenges that I didn't face. The built-in babysitters I envied also meant that my girlfriends had many voices giving their opinions on how to raise their children. And there was the simple fact of time: my friends both had many more commitments than Dave and I did.

During that period, we also discovered that God had filled our lives with blessings—more than we could ever count. The absence of extended family had caused us to reach far and wide into our church community for mentors and companionship. Our need to rely on friends to make life work broke us of our independent streak and made us value the growth that comes from humility and vulnerability.

The Lord lifts up those who bow down, indeed.

Step #3: Ignore everybody

In my research on comparisons, I thought there might be a connection between comparisons and creativity. After all, if we are so busy frantically swinging our heads around to figure out what everybody else is doing, we are less likely to tap into the creative and unique in each of us. I didn't have to look further than my denim and white skinny jeans comparisons to see an utter lack of creativity happening when comparisons rule.

I headed to Google, and then to my library, where I found a book called *Ignore Everybody and 39 Other Keys to Creativity.*[1] The book was funny, but my favorite takeaway was the title. What if my rule for life was to stop comparing and start ignoring?

The apostle Paul touches on this "ignore everybody" rule in his second letter to the church at Corinth:

> We do not dare to classify or compare ourselves with some who commend themselves. When they measure themselves by themselves and compare themselves with themselves, they are not wise. We, however, will not boast beyond proper limits, but will confine our boasting to the field God has assigned to us, a field that reaches even to you. (2 Corinthians 10:12-13, NIV)

Just as Jesus used agrarian themes to appeal to his listeners in the Judean countryside, Paul used a runner's theme in his letters to Corinth, a city renowned for its track-and-field competitions. The Corinthians would have understoond what Paul meant about the field God had assigned to each of them. Like at a modern-day track meet, the ancient Corinthians prepared for a sprint or a chariot race marked out in their lane or blocked out in a starting gate. Even in those days, people tended to compare themselves with others, so Paul had to remind his readers to "stay in their own lanes." As the writer of one commentary noted, "The picture Paul has in mind is that of a course measured out by God for each of His servants—and, more particularly here for each of His apostles."[2]

You are on your own field, in a course marked out for you in advance. This competition is between you and the you God wants you to be. If you want to compare yourself, why don't you ask God about the you he sees you can be.

Step #4: Direct your sight

I love Jesus for many reasons, but I really *like* what an awesome storyteller he is. The way he whips out the perfect parable as a response to someone's heart issues is inspiring. The way those same parables still ring true thousands of years later is miraculous.

Take the parable of the vineyard workers, found in Matthew 20. We catch up with Jesus on a teaching and healing streak, as the intensity of his ministry builds not long before his death and resurrection. Jesus is a heart guy. On every occasion when someone—a leader, rich person, religious teacher—asks him about how he reads the law, he always comes back with a challenge to examine the heart. In this case, he uses a story to illustrate that God's economy doesn't work like ours.

> *When evaluating your own life, the only comparison you should make is between you now and the you God wants you to be.*

In the story, a landowner goes to the town square to hire day laborers to work his field. Presumably it's harvesttime, and the landowner will need many hands to pick the grapes at their peak.

Early that morning, the landowner agrees to pay a group of workers a denarius for their day's work. The text doesn't make it clear, but it's interesting that the original workers probably *asked or negotiated* for that wage.

For whatever reason (more work than he expected, the workers weren't that productive, or everyone slowed down), the landowner returns to the town square throughout the day to hire more workers. After three hours, he tells his newest hires that he'll pay them "whatever is right" (NIV). He goes out three more times to get more workers—but never mentions pay again. The landowner just tells them to come and work, and they do.

Intermission: Have I told you that I love how Jesus uses relatable language and settings for his readers? I've never been a day laborer or picked grapes for the harvest, but I do know something about finding a good deal at Designer Shoe Warehouse. Before I tell you the end of this parable, let's see if bringing the story into a modern-day setting helps you relate even more to it.

A DSW PARABLE

You've spent the last three hours in DSW, prowling for that perfect pair of shoes, the kind of shoes that are an anchor for every outfit, a signature of your style. It's fifteen minutes before closing time, and you've happened upon an amazing pair of leather boots with the perfect heel—in the clearance section!

At 60 percent off, they are in your budget, and you are thrilled. You slide them on; they feel like home, and you just have to wear them right out of the store. Ready for incredible? The shoes are only going to cost you fifty dollars. Singing the "Hallelujah Chorus" under your breath, you hop into the line, clicking your new boot heels together to the beat of the Muzak coming from overhead.

In line with you are several women who clearly don't value the dollar as you do. The first goes through the line with four pairs of amazing stilettos, some outrageous Italian brand that you wouldn't dare touch. *That's got to be an entire paycheck of shoes,* you think to yourself.

"Today," the register woman says, "you owe only fifty dollars." *What?* You know you didn't see the purple clearance sticker on *her* shoes! *How could that be?*

The next woman comes through with two pairs of running shoes that cost about $100 each. You know because you craned your neck around the line to find out what would happen next. "Today," the register woman says, "you owe only fifty dollars."

Wow! You are pumped, thinking about what kind of discount you'll get for your pair. You are waiting for a camera crew to jump out of somewhere because this generosity is ridiculous. As you approach the register, the woman says, "Today you owe only fifty dollars."

Your mouth drops. "Whaaat?? That's what my pair of boots are *marked*," you grumble. Your eyes narrow with envy as you check out the Italian-brand shoeaholic who went first. *Humph,* you think to yourself, *I need to talk to a manager.*

"The Hallelujah Chorus" forgotten, you stomp over in your new boots to the manager standing by. "Excuse me," you say as you tap her on the shoulder. "I worked hard to find these boots on sale, and then when it was time to pay, everyone in front of me owed the same amount as my clearance item. You made us all equal."

The manager turns to you. "Friend, am I being unfair to you? Didn't you agree that those shoes were worth what you were going to pay for them? If I decide to give those women their shoes for the same price, *what's it to you?*"

WORD UP

In the Matthew 20 parable, the vineyard workers come to get their wages at the end of the day. The landowner pays them, beginning with the ones hired last. They each get a denarius. The lunchtime guys each get a denarius. And then—as agreed upon—the full-day workers each get a denarius. As you would expect, comparisons begin. Grumbling breaks out. And the workers who sweated in the fields all day long are unhappy.

After the customer service manager, er, the landowner, explains himself, he slam-dunks the whole point home: "Are you envious because I am generous?"

How easy it is for us to fall into the comparison trap! Take my DSW example. Clearance-boot girl was perfectly happy to pay fifty dollars for footwear she wanted and loved—until she compared herself to the other girls in the line.

TEMPTED TO COMPARE?

Try these strategies instead:

- When you think, *I wish I were more like him/her*, replace this thought with *I'm only seeing a small sliver of this person's life.*

- When you feel resentment toward another, pray "Lord, give me eyes to see where I need to change my ways."

- When you wish for something you don't have, fix your eyes on what you do have. Keep your eyes on your own bag.

- Go with Romans 12:15: "Rejoice with those who rejoice." Make the conscious choice to humble yourself and ask the Holy Spirit to give you a heart that is joyful in others' joy.

- Foster creativity. Make a conscious effort to pursue activities you love. Paint pictures. Swing on the monkey bars. Take hip-hop. Ignore everybody else and create!

- Take action: Look at the list on pages 129–130. Write down two or three things that you feel grateful for in each area of potential comparison. The next time you feel tempted to compare, repeat to yourself an area of gratitude.

- Remember the landowner's question: "Are you envious because I am generous?" (Matthew 20:15, NIV). Don't disrespect God's generosity to you by ignoring his gifts because they don't seem to compare with those he has given to others.

Remember our Sunday school candy story? When those kids received their individual gifts, they were ecstatic. When they compared, they grumbled and complained. They were envious and resentful of those around them. They missed the joy of the gift because it was soured by ingratitude.

The point of the Sunday school candy exercise was this: keep your eyes on your own bag. God has given us each great gifts, which will become obvious if we are willing to accept them with gratitude. The parable of the vineyard workers and the DSW sale is the same. Focus on what God has given you rather than what you don't have. Remind yourself that he is your Maker. He formed you and created you just as you are, to do good works that he planned in advance for you to do. He wants you the way he made you. He saw you and called his work good.

It may be time to go to God to fix your sight—to make sure you see your gifts as he provided them, rather than pining over what you think they should be. What happens next is almost magical. You will begin to feel grateful for things you ignored. Your heart will begin to expand as you welcome others' blessings into your life, rather than simmering and stewing about them having it better than you do.

Changing my view helped me trash comparisons for good. In my comparison recovery, I've found that places of struggle are opportunities for God to show his transforming power. By keeping my eyes on my own bag, I've discovered the vast blessings that God has given me. When I consider the question, "Are you envious because I am generous?" I better understand what God is saying to me. My life may not look exactly the way I planned, but I'm grateful. God should stay king. He does a much better job of managing my life than I do.

Choose to let comparisons go.

SPACE BAR

A PRAYER

Dear God, it's so easy to miss the gifts you've given me! I'm sorry for the ways that I disregard and disrespect the woman you've made me to be. Today, I choose gratitude instead of comparisons, and I ask you to help me not only love you, but like who you've made me to be! Amen.

A JOURNALING EXERCISE

Comparisons and gratitude occupy the same place in our hearts. The more of one, the less room there is for the other. Quit the comparison game with this challenge: Can you find one hundred things to be grateful for? Make a list. Be as specific as "the color of the sky during yesterday's sunset" and as broad as "family." Try to pay special attention to the areas of your life where you are prone to compare.

_____

_____

_____

_____

_____

_____

_____

_____

_____

_____

_____

_____

_____

FOR GROUP DISCUSSION

1. This chapter touches on the parable of the vineyard workers.
   Read the parable in Matthew 20:1-16. What is your reaction to
   the landowner's generosity? How might his generosity and some
   of the workers' resentment be playing out in your own issues
   with comparison?

2. The moral of the Sunday school candy lesson was "Keep your eyes
   on your own bag." When you look in your own bag, what gifts from
   God do you see?

3. How has comparison affected your relationships? If comparing were
   not part of your life, how do you think your significant relationships
   might be different?

4. How would you describe the "field" God has marked out for you?

Nicole shows you how to stop comparing yourself to others and find your
own unique path. Snap the code with your smartphone or visit the link
below.

www.tyndal.es/ShesGotIssues8

CHAPTER 9

KNOW FEAR; NO FEAR?

Never be afraid to try something new.
Remember, amateurs built the ark; professionals built the Titanic.

UNKNOWN

I OFTEN MAKE SNAP DECISIONS based on adorability. Like the patent green heels that had me at hello—adorable, except they make my pinkie toes bleed. Or the puppy we adopted just as my family life began to settle into a routine. Adorable? Yep. Eats shoes, toys, and plastic dinosaurs like a rabid goat? Double yep.

After whirlwind years of pregnancy, our new normal was a little less new and a little more normal. I seemed a little less crazy, although I should perhaps verify that fact with my husband. After spending every waking moment meeting somebody else's needs for several years, the new schedule that revolved around school-age children was most welcome.

And it was into this normal that five wriggly pounds of puppy literally plopped into our yard.

My neighbor was fostering the puppies, nursing them back to

health after a traumatic beginning. One morning as the puppies rumble-tumbled over each other as if they had materialized off the pages of *The Poky Little Puppy*, she whispered conspiratorially to me, "I'm going to keep one brother if you keep the other." Faster than you can say "puppy chow," I was sold.

Other than his habit of eating toys, life with Shep the pup wasn't as crazy as I would expect—except for one thing. Shep had a penchant for sneaking out the front door. As we loaded up for preschool in the morning, Shep would beat my son through the door every time. It became commonplace to see a member of my family stomping down the cul-de-sac, wildly swinging an empty leash and yelling for the dog. Shep would make a beeline for his brother Scamp's house. He would skedaddle up the steep brick steps and then sit at the front door, looking expectantly at the doorknob, just waiting for it to turn and the door to open so he could play with his brother. This was cute but annoying and could have ended up very badly. So we got an invisible fence.

I wish I had a home video of Shep running into that invisible fence for the first time. I have never seen a more vivid illustration of what fear can do in our lives if we allow it to rule.

Shep had been prepared by our trainer, David, an avid out-doorsman with the ability to call dogs from miles away with the sound of his deep, rumbling voice. He pointed out the white marker flags to Shep and told him to stay away. But when the fence was finally activated, Shep made his normal leap for Scamp's door and received his first shock. He leapt back from the boundary as if one of his legs had been chopped off. Then he stopped in the middle of the yard and lay down. He seemed paralyzed by fear, unwilling to move at all. When we finally persuaded him to get up, he scurried to the front steps. We tried to coax him off, but he was having none of it. He created a rule for himself after that first shock. If he stayed on the sidewalk or steps, he was safe.

David came back to show Shep how much freedom he truly had. He brought his own dog with him, who managed to coax Shep off the steps and into the yard. But Shep associated David with the sting of the first shock. It was clear he didn't trust him and was in no hurry to get back into the grass or anywhere near him.

David and I worked together, using treats and affection to win Shep over and slowly, slowly show him how far his boundaries truly extended. Slowly, Shep's tail began to wag. Slowly, he explored his new boundaries.

Shep loves to bound around the front yard now. He loves the freedom of coming in and out of the house, and I love not chasing him around the neighborhood. But putting those limits into his life brought a little bit of pain and a lot of fear. Shep needed encouragement to know whom to trust—and how to follow them into the boundaries set up for him.

Fear in our lives has the potential to make us lie down like Shep, paralyzed into rigidity, living a life that seeks comfort over risk and security over growth. Many of our fears come naturally. Like Shep, we've felt the sting of life and it hurts. "I used to be completely carefree," one friend wrote in an e-mail. "My thought was if it was my time [to die] then that is what God wanted. Now I always worry about worst-case scenarios and think I can limit my risks. It is a constant struggle that I pray about daily."

Most of us have met a painful enough experience somewhere along the way that we know what fear feels like. But what we often struggle with is what we are to *do* with it. Those fears often mutate into a generalized sense of anxiety that can cripple our lives. Like Shep, we get zapped at some point and then choose to stay in one little corner of the great yard God has laid out for us. We feel unsure of our boundaries, and we don't trust the One who allowed us to get shocked in the first place.

If there is one issue that affects women more often than any other, it is fear and the subsequent anxiety that accompanies it. So together, let's uncover some of the reasons we do what we do and feel what we feel. Only then will we be ready to truly heal from our fear and run free in the boundaries God has set for us.

THE ANXIETY PROBLEM

Recent statistics report that almost forty million Americans suffer from anxiety—almost 18 percent of the population! Many forms of anxiety are much more common in women than in men.[1] Anxiety is defined as an exaggerated sense of fear or worry, beyond what would be expected for the situation. If severe enough, anxiety causes a crippling inability to work, live, and relate to people in meaningful ways. The problem of anxiety is compounded because it is often a "secret shame," one that most Christians feel they would not be dealing with if they were truly following Christ. Because of that, even severe anxiety often goes untreated and unrecognized, creating misery for them and their families.

The problem of anxiety is compounded because it is often a "secret shame," one that most Christians feel they would not be dealing with if they were truly following Christ.

No one escapes anxiety at some point in life, but we can sink so deeply into our worry that we lose touch with how much of an issue it truly is in our lives. So what's your relationship with anxiety?

YOUR RELATIONSHIP WITH FEAR AND/OR ANXIETY

Answer yes or no to the following statements[2] based on your experiences over the last three months:

1. I have experienced physical symptoms, such as dizziness, heart pounding, hands trembling, or feeling hot and/or flushed when overcome by worry.

    ＿＿ yes   ＿＿ no

2. I've had a panic attack, an overwhelming sensation that lasted from several minutes to several hours, when I felt as if I couldn't breathe and felt as if I might be having a heart attack.

    _____ yes   _____ no

3. I feel restless or on edge more days than not.

    _____ yes   _____ no

4. I've noticed that my sleeping or eating habits have changed because of feeling stressed out or worried.

    _____ yes   _____ no

5. More days than not, I feel unable to concentrate or as if I'm in a fog.

    _____ yes   _____ no

6. I have a specific fear (e.g., of germs, social settings, public speaking, etc.) that impedes my ability to function normally when confronted with that situation.

    _____ yes   _____ no

7. I have a specific fear that creates anxiety I can relieve only by certain actions or rituals, such as checking locks or stoves, thinking a certain way, or preparing certain foods.

    _____ yes   _____ no

8. I experienced a significant trauma (e.g., accident, illness, abuse) sometime in my past that gives me recurring nightmares, intrusive thoughts, or leads me to avoid certain people and places.

    _____ yes   _____ no

9. I am jumpy or easily agitated without cause.

    _____ yes   _____ no

Answering yes to any of these statements indicates you are dealing with anxiety. Most of us struggle with some anxiety—and this chapter and the next will help. But if you answered yes to many of the questions, or recognized a behavioral pattern that is significant, growing, or has lasted several months, you may struggle with an anxiety disorder.

Many people leave anxiety disorders untreated, assuming their lack of faith is the problem and that they need to keep quiet and get through it on their own. But the truth is, anxiety needs to be brought to the light before it can be addressed. Yes, God can help, and he will. But he's also the creator of medication, counseling, and healthy living—all of which he can use to help you improve your life.

Don't forget the first tenet of this book: "You've got issues." We all do! And if your issue is anxiety that is significantly impairing your life, there is help. One of the best things you can do for yourself, for your family, and for the community you are in is to face your anxiety head-on and deal with it. Not because you are bad for having it, but because doing so can bring you great freedom—and you may be just the person to lead others out of the same bondage. At the end of the book, you'll find some additional resources and help.

"NORMAL" ANXIETY

If you answered yes to only a few of the assessment questions, this is good news! But read on: severe anxiety can impede and cripple life, but low-lying anxiety can also be a symptom of a great spiritual struggle with fear, mistrust, or faith.

All of us experience some level of anxiety in life, because there are fears in this world that are common to all humanity. These fears cause feelings of anxiety, and often we act on those feelings. Acting on anxiety looks like a brooding thought life, a worrisome way of dealing with relationships, and a lack of vulnerability and openness with others. While we may be able to disguise these fears from other people and even ignore the feelings fear generates inside us, they will keep us from living with as much freedom as would be otherwise possible. For that reason, these are issues worth considering. How much do you relate with the following four common fears?

Fear of suffering

It is in our nature to avoid death and to try to keep ourselves from harm. Our senses of taste and smell, for instance, are hardwired to keep us from ingesting poison and to alert us to avoid smoke. We buckle our seat belts, wash our hands after sneezing, and avoid going for a mile-long swim in the ocean during a hurricane warning out of a reasonable sense of caution.

However, the line between common sense and unreasonable fear is a thin one. One person's foolishness is another's fun (for proof, look no further than bungee jumping). Likewise, we all make decisions in life out of a desire to avoid pain. Yet activities that one person stays away from to spare herself pain may be embraced by another person who views that pain as tolerable discomfort (for proof, look no further than marathons and natural childbirth).

No wonder we get confused about what's normal and what's not!

When we're driven by the fear of suffering, we spend an incredible amount of energy avoiding situations that might cause pain. Consider the time and money that go into "babyproofing" a home. If you headed to your local baby store and purchased every device that promised freedom and safety, you'd have a lock on every toilet for fear of drowning. You'd have a two-step device covering every outlet for fear of electrocution. Every entrance would be blocked by a baby gate for fear that baby might trespass into un-babyproofed areas. Every sharp corner would be covered in foam for fear of stitches, every faucet wrapped for fear of burns. Every feeding item would be BPA-free for fear of poisoning, every toy plastic-free for fear of cancer. Every breakable would be out of reach for fear of shattering; every object that could pass through a toilet-paper roll would be thrown away for fear of choking. Every bed would have no covers for fear of smothering; and every bedside equipped with a bed rail for fear of falling. And of course every cabinet would be well locked for fear of anything else not mentioned here!

I am exhausted! Writing that wore me out, and living it sure would. Let's suppose for a minute that you approach life as the above paragraph describes. I would guess two things about you. First, you are exhausted and joyless. Living with this level of vigilance makes it impossible to relax. Without times when you stand down from being on guard, you end up seeing only the potential for pain in life—without any of the joy. Second, you are deceived. You have bought into the lie that you can control all situations in life where pain may exist. True, it is within our power to manage our risks—but we cannot eliminate them.

In addition to the fear of death, many of us fear emotional pain. We've never reckoned with the dark side of our hearts and don't know how to deal with our negative emotions. We feel the pain of loss or betrayal. We feel the darkness of anger and frustration. But when's the last time someone encouraged us to stay with those negative emotions? When's the last time we welcomed those feelings?

What's your tolerance level for pain in life?

So often we present a happy face on the outside yet nurse difficult feelings privately. If we haven't learned to create space for those negative emotions and to welcome God into those dark places, we often try to escape from them altogether. And some of our greatest fears are those that involve powerful and negative feelings.

Caitlin came to see me because she needed a safe place to figure out why she felt so dry and burned out at age twenty-four. As a leader in ministry, Caitlin felt like it was her job to keep it together, so my small office with a locked door seemed like the only place to truly be herself. After she had spilled out the story of her soul like the pieces of a giant jigsaw puzzle, we spent many hours together picking up pieces, examining them, and putting them back together. But several sessions in, something about her story nagged me. Like the jigsaw puzzle, her story felt only two-dimensional.

One day I asked her to draw a picture, which is sometimes what counselors do when they don't know what else to suggest. Caitlin brought the picture back the next week. She had drawn a torso, and in it she had placed colors and words, sprinkled down the arms like bracelets. But in the middle, near the heart, she had left everything blank. I asked her why it was empty in the middle. She shrugged and tucked her legs under her. She stared at me, and I stared at her, until the silence was uncomfortable and she said, "I should have just colored it all black."

Over the next few weeks, the "all black" of the middle of Caitlin's portrait became the very part that made Caitlin's story full-dimensioned. Caitlin slowly, carefully, painstakingly found words for the black. As we talked together, we uncovered the truth: Caitlin's understanding of being a good Christian girl allowed no place in her heart for negative and powerful feelings like fear, resentment, grief, and rage.

In recognizing the negative emotions that existed *whether Caitlin acknowledged them or not*, the black emptiness in the middle of her soul started to fill. And during that good but painful process, Caitlin realized that negative emotions aren't to be feared but are often a place where we can experience God's light, which always overpowers even the darkest places in the soul.

Fear of failure

Google returned more than eight million hits when I typed in "fear of failure." It's written about and quoted about extensively: "We have nothing to fear but fear itself." "Choose hope over fear."

Our collective consciousness agrees that making decisions based on fear should be avoided and that courage should always trump passivity. Perhaps we surround ourselves with these sayings because we live every day to avoid the feeling that we tried, put ourselves out there completely, and didn't cut it. We weren't good enough. We actually couldn't do it.

Failure flies in the face of the cultural messages that say, "You can do anything!" Failure spits on stories we tell our kids about "working hard to make it."

Determined to avoid failure at any cost, some of us make only safe decisions about life. We ignore the yearnings in our heart for more and stick with what's neither exciting nor uncomfortable. We don't take the leap of faith because we fear the skinned knees of trying and not making it the first time. And we fear what could also end up on the other side of trying and trying again—ultimate rejection.

Those of us who do stretch ourselves will fail at some point— whether at work, at friendships, or at love. But because acknowledging failure requires us to dig deep for something beyond ourselves, a different kind of character, we often refuse to acknowledge we've fallen flat on our faces.

I have become intimately acquainted with failure in my attempts to write this book. Many times, the writing journey felt like taking multiple spins on the Scrambler, that old double-circling, vomit-inducing carnival ride. Before every conversation with a publisher, I would hold on tight for a dizzying spin of hopes and possibilities, only to be flung off the ride in rejection. I would (with the help of my literary agent) limp my way back on the ride, repeating it all again.

I sat with my parents one day at lunch and asked, "Does ambition always have to end in failure?" I wondered if the true heroes are those who always push for the next dream and always dream bigger until they fail. I wondered if that would be the ultimate truth of my writing life. And I seriously doubted my ability to handle a lifelong Scrambler ride. It was too late to play it safe—I gave up on that when I launched this project into the world. But it wasn't too late to decide that skinning my knees hurt too much and I was done trying. And it wasn't too late for me to let a part of my soul die and insist that I never really wanted to write this book in the first place. These are the decisions we make in failure. We face the pain of giving up dreams or the pain of trying again.

The irony of failure and the pain it can bring is this: failure might be God's ultimate expression of himself—his reminder that we are not, in fact, in control of everything. Powerful fears call for a mighty God. They remind us of the puniness of our own strength. And it's often in the pain of the skinned knee and the crushed spirit where we experience that God is truly all we need.

Fear of rejection

Another fear also creates paralysis. We fear uncovering our true selves, allowing others to see who we really are—and then being rejected. Nothing speaks to this more than heartbreak. Do you remember your first crush? Remember that feeling of attraction and wonder? Remember wanting so badly for him to be entranced by who you really were—the essence of you—not just your appearance—and wanting him to really "get" you and then love you all the more? It doesn't matter if you were ten or twenty-two when it first happened. You and I have an inner yearning for that ultimate expression of belonging.

But the truth hits hard. Perhaps that love pulled away once he saw who you really are. Even if you ended up marrying that same first love, there will always be the inevitable feeling of rejection when things don't go according to plan. It may come in the sting of your loved one's withdrawal of love and affection after an argument. It may follow his inability to understand why you are so hurt by something he did with the best of intentions.

This painful yearning of uncovering ourselves and then being spurned or misunderstood leads to one of the deepest levels of pain for our human hearts. This is why I always took breakups seriously in counseling—even when the girl was in middle school. Oh, the pain of rejection cuts so deeply! And if we don't reckon with our pain and invite the only One who will never forsake us into that place, we may keep ourselves covered and never risk letting anyone see the real essence of ourselves again.

Like Shep in the front yard, once we have been shocked after putting ourselves out there, we may retreat to the very small area where we feel safe. We may choose to expose only certain parts of ourselves that we deem acceptable, parts of us that haven't been rejected. We stake our identity on the power of our intelligence or the shape of our body or our ability to be "the life of the party." In doing so, we begin to actually reject part of ourselves—the parts that feel needy or unfinished. Sometimes we become human chameleons, changing our stripes and colors and preferences to mirror the one we want acceptance from. We put a tourniquet on the parts of us that feel unacceptable, squeezing the life out of whatever feels needy or different or unfinished. We reject parts of ourselves to avoid human rejection so as to avoid our deepest fear of all—the fear of being alone.

Fear of being alone

Theologian Paul Tillich said that "language . . . has created the word 'loneliness' to express the pain of being alone. And it has created the word 'solitude' to express the glory of being alone."[3] Most of us have experienced both the great agony of loneliness and the yearning to be alone. When we are single, we fear being alone for life. When we are married, we fear being left alone by the death of our husband. When we have children, we fear being left by them as they grow. Choosing love means reckoning with the fear of being left.

When I'm evaluating the emotional or spiritual health of a woman, one of my favorite questions is how she feels about being alone. Not "alone" as in watching TV or obsessing on Facebook. I mean alone, like choosing solitude. Her response to that answer is always instructive. When a person avoids solitude at all costs and finds it painful, I often sense she is very unhappy with herself.

Unchecked, the fear of being alone causes us to give up portions of ourselves to avoid loneliness at all costs. We surround ourselves with noise—entertainment, media, diversions, people—so that we can avoid the inner emptiness that being alone often brings to the surface. Yet drowning out feelings of loneliness closes us off from more than our true selves; it prevents us from allowing Jesus to fill those places of emptiness with his presence and his peace. Solitude, it turns out, is fertile ground for sowing a deeper, richer relationship with Christ.

FEAR VS. ANXIETY

All of us deal with fear. It's commonplace to assume that we can let fear hang out in our souls without causing any problems. It's as if we have a permanent waiting room for our emotions that don't need to be dealt with. But believe me, while these emotions can remain submerged for a while, they won't wait forever. So when we struggle with fear—real fear—eventually we will have to respond to it. Anxiety is often our response to fear, our desire to *do something* about the fears we have.

As I began writing this chapter, a dear friend of mine was in a car accident. I had an immediate fear: that she would die or be paralyzed or mentally incapacitated for the rest of her life. I feared for her the pain of death—an imminent, immediate fear. I feared emotional pain for her, her family, and myself. These were true fears with a definitive cause.

The day of the accident, I rushed to visit my friend in the hospital. I left my children with their regular babysitter, yet I had an overwhelming urge to tell her not to drive the kids anywhere. She'd driven them around without incident for months, as had my babysitter before her and the one before her. But the fear kindled by my friend's accident demanded a response in my soul, a drive to do something with the feeling. This is anxiety. It is an irrational thinking pattern, often based on a rational fear. My response to my friend's car accident was to control what I could. In a wild flight of magical thinking, I allowed my real fear to blossom into controlling, irrational behavior.

Exploring why we fear is most certainly the first step to understanding our anxiety—that sense of nervous anticipation we live with in an attempt to avoid feeling or dealing with the root cause of our fear. We can find comfort in knowing there is a reason we are anxious!

If everyone deals with some sort of anxiety, you may be wondering, *is it really a problem worth addressing?* Yes, because anxiety is not just a feeling. When we experience fear or feel anxiety, we often take matters into our own hands to try to *relieve* that anxiety. We may go to great lengths to avoid leaving our children alone with a babysitter. Maybe we find ourselves grasping at friendships or relationships we shouldn't be in because our anxiety says "you can't be alone." Maybe we act out our fear of rejection by striving for perfection in our bodies, our food habits, or our achievements.

This relentless striving to relieve our anxiety forces us to remain focused on ourselves. And here is where fear becomes the problem. We miss opportunities to love, to grow, and to serve. We take the energy and passion God has put in us for change and we turn it

FEAR OR ANXIETY?

Do you know how to distinguish between fear and anxiety?

- **Fear:** An unpleasant emotion, fear is one of the most basic instincts. Fear is the dread of something immediate and dangerous. It is related to a specific object (e.g., fear of bees). We develop rational fear (e.g., fear of fire) to keep us alive. Irrational fear, which can keep us from living a free and full life, is also learned.

- **Anxiety:** A feeling of nervous anticipation of a future event or situation that seems uncontrollable or unavoidable, anxiety is often a response to fear, although it's not always directly related to the original fear object.

into a cycle of self-protection. We are unable to fully explore the boundaries set forth by God.

Thank God that his kind of love is not satisfied to leave us there! I imagine him saying to each of us as we come before his throne with our fears and worries:

Yes, child, I know why you fear. I've seen every tear you've cried. I know you and love you and understand you. But I am God, and with me, you will overcome. Nothing is too hard for me. Nothing is beyond my reach and no circumstance that has caused you to fear is greater than the love I have and the reasons why you should trust me.

We will never live the life God planned for us if we limit ourselves to the places we've deemed safe, ignoring the real boundaries God has put into place for us. Like Shep, we keep ourselves on the steps when life feels too dangerous. The rest of the world seems too daunting, and we decide our own self-appointed boundaries might be safer. Fortunately, God has given us quite a bit of freedom, and in the next chapter we'll explore how to tiptoe out of our safety zone and experience the exhilaration of the worry-free life.

SPACE BAR

A PRAYER

Father God, I'll just say it. I'm scared. Life is big and daunting and overwhelming. Daily I'm faced with news from the Internet and from friends of the real pain that life can bring. Sometimes I want to pull the covers over my head and hide out until heaven. But God, you've given me a purpose in this life, and you've told me, "Fear not!" no matter what comes my way. Would you help me, Lord, to see how you are working in my life through my issue of fear? Amen.

A JOURNALING EXERCISE

Take a mental inventory. Write at the top of your journal "What if . . . ?" Then spend ten minutes writing down every question that comes to mind after that statement.

_____

_____

_____

_____

_____

_____

_____

_____

FOR GROUP DISCUSSION

1. Before this chapter, did you believe you had a fear or anxiety issue? What about after?

2. Of the four fears listed, which do you struggle with most? Are there any you struggle with that are not listed?

3. What do you think is the difference between fear and common sense? How do you determine which one is at play when you make decisions?

4. What is your relationship with solitude? Is loneliness an issue for you? Remember, even the busiest and most "relatable" women often struggle with loneliness. In what ways do you feel unknown?

Nicole explains the difference between fear and common sense. Snap the code with your smartphone or visit the link below.

www.tyndal.es/ShesGotIssues9

CHAPTER 10

THE BIG LEAP FROM FEAR TO FREEDOM

What are you afraid of? Let God act. Abandon yourself to Him.
You will suffer, but you will suffer with love, peace, and
consolation. . . . You will weep, but your tears will be sweet,
and God Himself will come with satisfaction to dry them.

FRANÇOIS FÉNELON

"I COULDN'T JUST SIT THERE!" said the woman next to me as we both watched our sons at baseball camp. "I couldn't let that coach continue to ignore my son on the bench. He had him sit out three innings in a row while other players made error after error! What if my son started to hate baseball? What if he wouldn't play anymore? What if he missed his chance . . . ?"

I tried not to chuckle as I wondered if she wanted to say ". . . missed his chance to get drafted into the big leagues?" After all, our sons are eight years old and can't even cut their own meat. Seems a bit, well, premature to be worried about college scholarships or major-league signings. Despite how silly it seemed, the expression on the woman's face told me she was very serious. Living by what-ifs compelled her to complain to her child's coach, despite the expressed desire of her son and husband that she not do so.

"But I couldn't just sit there and watch it," she explained. I let her stew over her what-ifs as she and I turned back to watch our little boys toss baseballs.

Have you ever struggled with the tyranny of the what-if? I think most of our anxieties start with these two words. What if I get hurt? What if I fail? What if people reject me? What if I end up unknown, unloved, unheard? As the what-ifs of our hearts increase in volume and intensity, the pressure in our souls to do something about them also increases.

Yesterday my children were watching one of the most annoying cartoons ever created on DVD. They had smuggled that DVD into the car like a razor on an airplane, and there I was, stuck listening to this cartoon blare over the speakers. I lived with the incessant chatter of the cartoon for a few minutes, but the barrage of voices was overwhelming.

Those chattering voices remind me of the what-ifs that run through our minds. When they go unchecked, these internal voices run endlessly through various scenarios, spinning the same thoughts over and over, running like a hamster on a wheel in our mind. Anxiety is like a pressure cooker in our souls. The pressure of the what-ifs builds, and if the fears aren't faced, eventually we are ready to burst.

Finally the cartoon voices in our car got to be too much to handle. I gave my kids a two-minute warning and then powered down the DVD. Ah, blessed calm and silence! The ten seconds before my kids started arguing were bliss.

Wouldn't it be wonderful if we could turn off anxiety as quickly as a cartoon? Of course it's not that easy, but with God's help, we can give anxiety a two-minute warning and get that thought hamster off the wheel.

ANXIETY: A SIN?!?
Because anxiety is so prevalent in our culture and so rooted in legitimate fears, we often don't want to face the reality that anxiety

is a direct path to sin. (Sorry—as if there wasn't enough to worry about, we get worried about the truth that we sin when we worry!)

Anxiety is just another one of our issues. It's not a personality trait. It's not something we are born with. Even if we have a personality predisposed to fear, that is not an excuse to allow it to run (or ruin) our lives. Let us not take the truth of the situation as condemnation. Rather, let's view the scriptural passages on anxiety as instructive—they teach us that God will relieve our worries. And God doesn't just leave us at relief: he equips us to confront and defeat the anxiety in our souls.

Because we live in a less-than-perfect world, some anxious thoughts are inevitable. So when do our anxious thoughts become sin? When we allow the voice of anxiety to determine our thoughts, feelings, and actions. The object of our fear becomes the idol that we allow to determine our actions.

That's what happened to Pilate, the one who gave the order to crucify Jesus. It's clear that the Roman governor was intrigued and mystified by the time Jesus had been brought before him for questioning. Pilate's wife had told him earlier that he should leave Jesus alone (Matthew 27:19). On top of that, Pilate was convinced Jesus was innocent. However, Mark 15 indicates that Pilate was anxious for the people's approval.

My guess is that Pilate had staked his whole identity on obtaining power and position, and because he feared losing that approval, he refused to make the right choice, even when standing before God himself. This is the power fear can have in our lives, so I'm thankful God gives us so much instruction about how we should handle the issue of anxiety.

Authors Neil Anderson and Rich Miller write:

More than 300 biblical passages tell us not to fear, but little relief will come to someone struggling with phobias if he or she is just told not to fear. This is not a sufficient answer. Such behavioral and legalistic approaches only create more confusion and guilt. Although Christ is the answer, and the truth will set us free, the suffering saint needs to know *how* to connect with God and *how* the truth sets us free.[1] (italics mine)

Whether you fear pain, failure, rejection, or loneliness, there is only one path to true freedom. Friend, there is no other issue that will draw you as close to God, so often in your day, as the trouble of anxiety. If you've been a Sunday-morning or even an every-morning-with-God kind of woman, anxiety is an issue that will drive you into the arms of Jesus all day long.

I saw a client early in my counseling days who was your typical anxious girl. She worried about her schoolwork, her friendships, and her health. She had a sensitive disposition and seemed overly aware of how social situations were playing out. I wasn't surprised when I met her mother, who had learned to mask it a bit better but clearly struggled with the same concerns.

When I sat down with this mom, I asked her how she had dealt with her own anxiety over the years. She shared all kinds of techniques, from exercise to meditation to vitamins. I asked her if there was a time when she felt less anxiety than usual. She looked away for a minute, then looked back. "You know, there was . . ." she started. "It was when my counselor 'prescribed' that I spend an hour with God every morning. A whole hour! And I actually did it. I have never been so peaceful. Huh."

We chuckled together that here she sat, in another counseling office, remembering that her anxiety was not addressed by paying a counselor but by experiencing the free, invaluable presence of God by spending an hour with him each day.

I realize that this is the stock Christian answer. You may be frustrated by the lack of "how" in this prescription. But after asking numerous women to share their journeys in anxiety, I'm realizing that this is the simple truth: the more worry is a part of your life, the more opportunities you have to spend with God.

WORD UP

Let's cannonball into God's Word and see what he says about the four main fears we all face.

Freedom from pain: rolling in the deep

If you read the Bible specifically to glean what you could about avoiding pain, you might find yourself dismayed: no person in Scripture escaped the pain of this life. Every character, from Adam to Jesus, experienced physical, emotional, or spiritual pain. Here we find our first truth: suffering is inevitable.

But the second truth may be more astounding than the first. Suffering seems to have a prominent place on God's canvas of life. Perhaps pain is the way God gets our attention. Not because he is a sadist but because he has a view of our lives and souls that is eter-

Suffering is inevitable.

nal, and he is first and foremost concerned that our hearts align with his. If we treasure earthly things above all else, we will have no choice but to conclude that God is mean. How could a good God allow child molestation or cancer or tragic natural disasters? You see, if we keep our eyes focused on earth as if this were heaven itself, we will find ourselves quickly disillusioned.

Thankfully God reminds us that this life is not all there is. Throughout Scripture God refers to the transitory nature of our human lives: "We blossom like a flower and then wither" (Job 14:2). Solomon says in Ecclesiastes 2:3, "While still seeking wisdom, I clutched at foolishness. In this way, I tried to experience the only happiness most people find during their brief life in this world." He experienced the double-minded struggle of seeking to escape pain on earth while still trying to keep eternity at the center of his mind. This describes our struggle as we make sense of pain.

Jesus says, "I tell you not to worry about everyday life—whether you have enough food and drink, or enough clothes to wear" (Matthew 6:25). Stop for a minute and consider how preposterous that statement is. Jesus tells us that we need not be concerned about the most basic of our needs. Because I live in a country of plenty, these words just roll off my tongue. But Jesus delivered this message to the poor, people who had to work very hard just to scrape by! And he consistently pointed them—and us—to a whole new level of life.

The apostle Paul writes a beautiful passage in 1 Corinthians 15 that calls us to a new perspective when we are in pain. He repeatedly urges us to feel and experience the truth that Jesus Christ experienced victory over death and offers us a resurrection life. Although we experience pain, it has lost its "sting" compared to what death meant to us without Christ. So how does this affect our lives? We realize that:

- pain is still a part of our reality—but it is not the ultimate reality;
- pain will still hurt—but it cannot kill our souls;
- pain will come, and even be allowed by God—but he will always use it for his glory.

God will play the ultimate trick on evil by using what was meant for bad and transforming it into something that leads others to recognize his existence and to worship him. How's that for amazing?

These words alone may seem inadequate for the pain you are facing. But if you do not have a bedrock of truth to stand on, you cannot begin to face your fear. You and I must drill into our souls the truth that this world is not the end! Everything around us screams, "Eat, drink, and be merry, for tomorrow you die!" But death is not the end for the Christian—it is the beginning. When we see our earthly lives as merely one stop on our eternal journey, when we get a taste of what heaven will be like through experiencing worship or God's presence even for a moment, we see that every pain is really just a momentary trouble.

Freedom from the fear of failure: redefining success

Sometimes our fear of pain is compounded when we fear the pain of failure. Anytime we venture into new territory, be it with a job, a relationship, or even a new interest, we have to reckon with the giant of failure. And this one feels like such a Goliath! It towers over us, warning that we will not survive the crushing blow of defeat. So often we cower in its presence because our definition of success appears unattainable.

When I got the wild, rabid idea to write a book, there were many failures along the way. If my idea of failure was not getting a book contract within six months, then I failed. If my idea of failure was being rejected for an article or post I wrote in the hopes that an editor would hire me, then I also failed. And believe me, those rejections (plus many others) hurt! In order to continue to go after my idea, I needed to have a new definition of success.

I took comfort in the many stories of rejection that writers share. When I found out that Kathryn Stockett, author of the bestselling novel *The Help*, was rejected sixty times before an agent picked up her completed novel, I knew she must have something to teach us about redefining success in light of failure. Stockett explains her obsession and perseverance in the midst of failure:

> *To face failure, I need a new definition of success.*

The point is, I can't tell you how to succeed. But I can tell you how not to: Give in to the shame of being rejected and put your manuscript—or painting, song, voice, dance moves, [insert passion here]—in the coffin that is your bedside drawer and close it for good. I guarantee you that it won't take you anywhere. Or you could do what this writer did: Give in to your obsession instead.[2]

In the pain of rejection sixty times over, Stockett discovered the only thing worse than being rejected was not trying—the equivalent of death.

Sisters, so many of us walk around like the living dead because of our fear of trying and failing. Sadly we might conclude that the deadness we are experiencing is all life has to offer. We must redefine our definition of success in light of God's guidelines for our lives. First Corinthians 14:1 gives us a simple definition of a "successful" life: "Go after a life of love as if your life depended on it—because it does. Give yourselves to the gifts God gives you. Most of all, try to proclaim his truth" (*The Message*).

When we're unsure about why we are making a decision—to keep ourselves safe or because it is a good, prudent choice—we can ask ourselves three questions based on this verse:

1. Am I making this decision out of love or out of fear?
2. Am I pursuing—and using—the gifts God gave me?
3. Am I proclaiming truth? Do I know truth from God's Word? Do I live by it?

Especially when answering the first question, we must rely heavily on the Holy Spirit. Psalm 139:23-24 says "Search me, O God, and know my heart; test me and know my anxious thoughts. Point out anything in me that offends you, and lead me along the path of everlasting life." The Hebrew word for *anxious* here appears only in the plural in Scripture.[3] I take heart knowing that God never expects us to have only one anxious thought but knows that we have many! He instructs us to allow him to test our hearts. We don't have to come to him with it all figured out. Rather, we can invite him to do the searching and seeking, and then, even when our anxiety is rising, look forward to saying with the psalmist, "Your consolation brought joy to my soul" (Psalm 94:19, NIV).

Freedom from the fear of rejection: choosing God's approval

Our fear of rejection is the big what-if in our relational lives. What if they don't like me? Consider this testimony from one of my friends:

> I have always wanted people to like me. I can't remember a time in my life when I wasn't desperate for the affirmation of my parents and teachers and any adults in my life. I didn't have a history of abuse or anything, I just always felt this great need to be liked. As I got older, I realized that there were some things about girls that boys liked more. So I started dieting to be the "perfect" weight and I tried to always be exactly what a guy would want. This led to several bad relationships where I just morphed into whatever I perceived would make the guy "like" me. I didn't even know who "me" was at that point!
>
> Then my mentor pointed out that I was living a "vanilla" life—the flavor everyone likes but no one really loves. I didn't want to be vanilla anymore. And I knew that wasn't what God made me to be. For me, being free of my anxiety means reminding myself that God did not create me to be vanilla, and that the pinnacle goal of my life shouldn't—and can't—be for everyone to like me. In

a weird way, that's freed me to appreciate the people who love my non-vanilla self, and released the desire to have everyone like me the same.

My friend had to experience the loss of herself in her search for approval before she found out the truth of the way fear had clawed into the DNA of her soul. Perhaps this is a bit of what Jesus meant when he said, "If you try to keep your life for yourself, you will lose it. But if you give up your life for me, you will find true life" (Matthew 16:25).

If you think you can live a life for Christ and still have everyone like you, then I've got news for you: you are missing something! Jesus said it very plainly in John 15:18-19: "When the world hates you, remember it hated me before it hated you. The world would love you if you belonged to it, but you don't. I chose you to come out of the world, and so it hates you." Notice the use of "when"— as in "when the world hates you," not "if the world hates you"! This is shocking for my nice-Christian-girl stereotype! Shouldn't I want everyone to like me? But it won't happen. When you refrain from gossip, when you don't join in petty arguments, when you make decisions for you and your family that run contrary to culture, people will not like it. They will talk about you. They may even reject you.

But Jesus told his disciples and us: "Do you remember what I told you? 'A servant is not greater than the master.' Since they persecuted me, naturally they will persecute you. And if they had listened to me, they would listen to you! The people of the world will hate you because you belong to me, for they don't know God who sent me" (John 15:20-21).

Friend, your job isn't to make everyone like you. It's to glorify God with your life. That requires quieting your spirit so you can hear from God and be obedient when he speaks.

Recently I sensed God telling me to cancel everything on my family's social calendar for the next three weeks. I knew it was God, first of all, because I would never think that on my own. I usually say yes before a person even finishes asking me to do something! Canceling everything didn't mean backing out of a playdate or two for my family. Canceling everything meant forgoing a ministry trip, a family trip, and a camp for my son, not to mention those playdates. My skin crawled at the thought of disappointing so many people and reneging on my word. But even stronger than my distaste for being unliked was my distaste at ignoring God when he had so clearly made his presence known.

How do you know you are following God's voice? One sign, I believe, is when you sense a deep peace in obedience. So often we make choices to try to keep everyone happy—both God and people—but you'll know your decision is good by the peace in your heart. I didn't like canceling. But I (sometimes grudgingly) trust that God knows what is best for my life, even when I can't make people happy along the way.

Freedom from the fear of being alone: embracing solitude

We live in a quick-fix world that offers online dates and expensive fertility treatments. We've created entire industries that insist we can beat our worst fear: the fear of being ultimately and desperately alone. We hear the truth about ourselves most clearly in this place of aloneness; perhaps that's why we avoid it. We don't want to know the truth and so prefer to stay active with achievements, work, and relationships.

> We know we are seeking God's approval by the fruit of peace in our hearts.

Yet without the "quiet center," as Henri Nouwen calls it,[4] the very things we fill our time with become meaningless. When we do find ourselves alone, we have to confront the stripped-down version of ourselves, not the self that performs or achieves or relates or acts. It is inevitable that many of us will experience loneliness in solitude, but the great myth of our day is that having the right relationships will keep us from that loneliness. Some of the loneliest women I know are married. They have wonderful children and fulfilling careers, yet their spirits are not settled, nor have they discovered a "quiet center."

The journey to this center is perhaps the scariest journey we can take. To allow quiet. To allow the true abyss of our selfishness to come to the front of our awareness. To see ourselves as desperately needy and not at all worthy. Yet only in this place can we hear the crystal-clear truth of God's Word to us. That we are his beloved. That he knows our condition and loves us wildly in that place.

My friend Becca says, "In solitude we discover that our worth is not the same as our usefulness." This is the beautiful gift of solitude, and it's worth the loneliness required to get there. The paradox of solitude is that when we journey through loneliness, through the truth of ourselves, we find the sweetest communion with Jesus, the only One who can and will ever know us fully, completely, from the depths of our heart to the tips of our toes, and love us extravagantly just as we are.

Shawn McDonald sings a song that expresses this realization:

> *I need your love to carry me by.*
> *Would you come and fill this heart of mine,*
> *'Cause I can't do it alone. . . .*
> *Won't you come and fill my soul. . . .*
> *All I need is you, my God.*[5]

These words of surrender and trust are found only in a place of need and emptiness. But sweet, amazing time with Jesus awaits you if you are willing to take the journey.

You cannot make God show up by offering him a few minutes of solitude a couple of times before you give up. Stick with it, and take courage as you remember his promises in Scripture. He will:

- never fail you or forsake you (Deuteronomy 31:6)
- make peace for you through the sacrifice of Jesus (Romans 5:1)
- offer you fellowship with others through the Holy Spirit (Philippians 2:1-2)
- instruct others to care for you in your loneliness (1 Timothy 5)

If you are to find the peaceful center in the whirlwind of your life, you must find a place to experience the intimacy of God that comes from spending time alone with him. And when you find that place of communion, God will equip you for your life to come.

A YEAR WITHOUT FEAR

All of us fall prey to the trap of anxiety at one time or another. Perhaps we recognize it only when it sneaks up on us at the end of our day when we realize we've spent much of our thought life ruminating on a problem—and consequently very little time in prayer!

Maybe what we call prayers have turned into long to-do lists for God covering every worry and concern—and we've swept praise and worship to the side. So how exactly can we apply God's Word to combat anxiety? Jean's story gives us a dramatic picture of just what can happen when we allow Jesus to kick fear out of our lives. I'll let her say it in her own words:

> My saying no to fear started with a class I took to increase
> my training for a ministry job right after college. The
> class was focused on healthy personal relationships. As

weeks of classes passed, the effects that fear had on my life were more and more evident. Before the class I thought I was simply a shy and timid introvert. After, I was not so sure—it seemed fear permeated almost every aspect of my life.

I had real reasons to live in fear. Growing up, I found that my parents and siblings were not emotionally safe people. While I wasn't abused, my family was disinterested in me. Particularly during my teenage years, any academic disappointment, relational heartbreak, or any failure to achieve my own desires was processed by me alone, in a vacuum outside familial care.

My struggle was always centered around the opinion of others: being judged a failure, being embarrassed or rejected, and being afraid of intimacy. I never took chances unless I could ensure success. I loved to sing and wanted to try out for school musicals but never did. I knew I had leadership qualities but never ran for school office. I was a master at making excuses to avoid social gatherings—dates, parties, dances, and sleepovers. I pushed people away for self-protection.

Yet through a friend I started attending a youth group in high school. I soaked up devotional talks and Bible studies. I was the stereotypical kid with the "God-shaped hole in my heart." That there was a loving God with kind, tender, continual, powerful, active thoughts of me was (and still is) compelling. In the safety of a relationship with Jesus, I began to experience his healing work in my heart and mind.

It's now several years later, and I find myself in ministry. Through this class I made a commitment to ask Jesus to truly be Lord in all areas of my life. I decided to dedicate one year to saying yes to following Christ and no to following fear.

My choice to say no to fear started small. First, I told the story of how I came to know Christ at an outreach breakfast for high school students. I had a lot of 3 x 5 cards with every word carefully chosen and practiced. Voice shaky and knees weak to the point of collapse, I'm not sure if I made any sense. But I did it. And I did it again. I taught at large group meetings, tried leading songs, played guitar in large groups, and led retreats. I equated success with the attempt, not the mastery of the skill.

After a short time, I was so different! So I broadened my challenge beyond youth ministry. I gave reports at elder meetings, spoke in Sunday worship, became a worship leader, and led mission trips. Not only did my work life change, but my personal life did too. I began to participate in the singles ministry, went out on dates and on vacations with friends, and played in a sports league. And I met the man who would become my husband.

It would be a mistake to think I'm a brave woman who conquers her fears. In my heart and mind, this was an exercise in trusting Jesus—I chose to believe he would be with me as I said no to fear. As the year went on, the Lord showed up in each of these challenges. Every time! I took thousands of steps that year. Passages from Psalms 23, 37, 46, and 56, as well as Isaiah 40 and Hebrews 4, all became my own. I began to take ownership of the words written thousands of years ago, like they could have been written in my journal, such as Psalm 46:1-2, "God is our refuge and strength, an ever-present help in trouble. Therefore we will not fear . . ." (NIV). Or Psalm 37:23-24: "The LORD makes firm the steps of the one who delights

REPLACING ANXIETY WITH PEACE

1. When you find yourself ruminating, slowly repeat a Scripture verse to yourself. Consider memorizing verses that bring you peace, such as Exodus 14:14; Psalm 37:7; or Psalm 46:10. When your thoughts get stuck on one problem or situation, slowly repeat the verse until you are free from the anxious train of thought.

2. Use a breath prayer to replace anxious thinking. Try something like: *Father in heaven* (inhaling), *be my peace* (exhaling). Try to breathe deeply, letting your stomach rise and fall with each breath.

3. Create your own "year without fear" challenge in the spirit of Jean's story. What if you didn't allow yourself to say no because of fear?

4. Work on dialoguing with the what-ifs in your life. Ask God to be the voice that answers each of your what-ifs and guides you into confessing the fears that are restricting your life.

5. Take baby steps when facing fear. Try a little change before progressing to bigger things.

6. If you feel compelled to act on your anxiety, try to delay your response. For instance, if being in a public place makes you feel like you have to wash your hands, try to delay washing them for fifteen minutes. Ask God to give you the strength not to create rigid, unnecessary rules for yourself.

7. Consider progressive relaxation as a method to pray. (This is a great exercise to do before bed.) Lie quietly on the floor, facing up with palms up. Imagine yourself surrendering your worries to God. One by one, visualize your worry as an irritant on a body part. If you are worried about approval, picture that across your legs. Tense your legs up as tight as you can. As you release the muscles, also release that worry. Move up your body, tensing and relaxing as you breathe. Finally, take a mental scan of your entire body, checking to find any hidden tension or anxieties. Breathe and relax until you've given all your worries to God, handing them over like a basket of dirty laundry.

in him; though he may stumble, he will not fall, for the LORD upholds him with his hand" (NIV). It was all true, and I had a year's worth of experiences to prove it.

I didn't know Jean when she took a year to conquer fear. And without this story, I never would have known that fear once ruled her life. Jean is beautiful. Her story isn't without pain and suffering, but she lives out of freedom and joy. She accepts her weaknesses and her strengths. She knows what it means to live an authentic life, and she is a woman who lives with deep waters of stillness in her soul. Jean is a living testimony to the power of Christ to conquer all of our fears, and she serves as an inspiration for all of us who want to truly change. Jean's just an ordinary woman, like you and me, who's living in the modern miracle of transformation. Change is real, and God is ready. Are you?

SPACE BAR

A PRAYER

Dear heavenly Father, you are so clear with your words about fear! But somehow I need help making the leap from head knowledge about your Word to believing it's true in my heart. Lord, I want to trust you more, saying yes to your freedom and no to the fear that's crippling me. Help me to be honest and humble before you. Right now, I ask for your help, because I can't do this on my own. Show me the little or big steps I need to take to get free of any fears that keep me from the full life you have for me. Amen.

A JOURNALING EXERCISE

Look back at your journal exercise from the last chapter. Revisit your what-if page. Draw a line straight down the middle of a blank page.

On one side, write one of the scariest what-ifs from the last chapter. On the other, write as if a wiser, less-scared you is answering the what-if. What would that wiser, less-scared self say to the current what-if fear? What words would that wiser self use? What Scripture might she apply?

FOR GROUP DISCUSSION

1. Do you consider yourself to have an anxious personality? Why or why not?

2. Choose one verse to memorize about fear or anxiety.

3. What would change in your life if you chose to live a year without fear?

4. Have you had victory over any anxieties in your life? What has worked for you?

Nicole shares how God's Word can help you stop worrying so much. Snap the code with your smartphone or visit the link below.

www.tyndal.es/ShesGotIssues10

CHAPTER 11

ANGER IS FOR FOOLS LIKE ME

Anger is never without a reason, but seldom with a good one.
BENJAMIN FRANKLIN

I come from a long line of passionate women. When I called my mom to warn her that this chapter was coming, she told me about the time my grandmother threw every spice out of the spice drawer and across the kitchen because my mom hadn't put the cinnamon away. My grandmother and my mother both relate to transforming into rabid, howling hyenas faster than you can say, "Did you leave your hairbrush in the kitchen again?"

And so it's sort of funny that, on the morning I sat down to write this chapter, I had just gotten after my daughter because she couldn't find one of her new gymnastics hand grips (from the pair I had specially ordered and told her not to lose ten times). And last week, when I threw a block of parmesan cheese followed by the entire cheese grater at my husband after he made a comment about the mess in the house? Kind of funny. And a few years ago, when I kicked the trash can so hard I dented the metal, which stands as a memorial to the damage that anger can wreak on a household? Mildly amusing. I have more stories too. I think most of us do.

But these are not the things that get discussed at Mother's Day teas and women's retreats. Nostalgia about children growing up? Acceptable. Tears? Totally fine. But bitter, forceful anger? From nice Christian girls? Anger might turn women into wild things. Then again, anger causes some women to turn to all kinds of secretive behaviors to vent their true feelings.

No longer, ladies. Because anger has the power to change lives. Many of us know what it's like to be on the receiving end of rage in the form of emotional or physical abuse. Many of us also know what it is to speak and act from a place of anger ourselves. Yet anger can also change lives for the better—if it is harnessed and transformed into a power for good.

GETTING MADD

In 1980, one mother was grieving the unthinkable . . . the death of her thirteen-year-old daughter. While walking to a church carnival, Cari Lightner was struck by a hit-and-run driver. She was literally knocked out of her shoes, and her broken body was thrown 125 feet from the collision. The man who hit her was drunk, and he confessed only after his wife found their badly damaged car and he couldn't explain what had happened.

Cari's mom, Candy, was devastated. And then she got mad. Mad about injustice, about a lax legal system, and about a culture that looked away and laughed at drunk driving. So she gathered a small group of other grieving mothers together and decided to do something about the outrage of drinking and driving. With nothing but the force of their emotions, these women banded together and created "one of the great grassroots successes in American history."[1]

Mothers Against Drunk Driving is a testament to the power of using grief and anger to create positive change. American culture and legislation were forever changed by women who chose to take their grief and passion public, to take what we might call righteous anger and use its power for exactly what God has called us to be in this world . . . a voice for the voiceless. Candy Lightner got mad and used that force for change, starting in the office that had once been her daughter's bedroom. Anger changes lives.

We can all nod along with a story like Candy's. I get teary at the thought of so much pain and grief. I'm willing to be emotional about what's wrong in our world, particularly the damage we do to one another. But my own uneasy relationship with this emotion makes it easier just to ignore it totally. I really don't want to talk about what my anger does. I don't really want to reap the consequences. I don't want to face the reality that I act in ways that I hate and don't quite have a place in my soul to understand how and what God might think of this anger.

Last year, when our church leadership team announced to our women's ministry that we would be teaching on anger, a collective groan rose from the women, followed by shut-your-mouth silence. When I told a few neighbors I was writing about anger, I got the same groan-then-silence response. As I consider their reaction, I wonder if these women, like me, are recalling the last time they lost their temper. What they said and how they said it. What they squeezed, slapped, or threw in anger. I wonder if some of them are thinking about the space in their souls where unresolved anger lives, how they hide it and suppress it and try to ignore it, all the time wondering how and why they have such strong, seemingly irrational feelings, a force they can't quite reconcile with their concept of what it means to be a sweet Christian woman.

There's another kind of woman altogether. She's the one who claims never to get angry. These women worry me even more. True, they aren't inflicting damage on anyone else with their words or actions. But studies consistently show that women who repress their anger tend to have that poison leak into many areas of physical and mental health. In fact, one definition of depression is "anger turned inward." The truth is that every woman I've ever met has had some good reasons to be angry, as well as many completely irrational reasons to be angry (see cheese grater incident above).

This chapter would be very short if there was one solution to anger: don't ever feel it. But anger is a God-created emotion! Fourteen times in the Old Testament, God himself is called "angry." The Hebrew word used is similar to *snort*, as in a horse that snorts. I imagine God saying "Humph!" as the Israelites turn away from him, as Samson gives in to the sweet talk of Delilah, as King Solomon follows his own way. In the New Testament, we read of Jesus and the apostle Paul getting angry as well.

Clearly, our models of righteousness felt the emotion of anger. Therefore, we should not fear the emotion itself, nor should we attempt to live a life devoid of anger. What we do with that anger is the real challenge before us all.

The powerful force of anger has two benefits. One, it can serve as a warning light when something is wrong. It is a signal that all is not well and something is going on in our hearts that needs to be examined. Two, anger can be the power that activates us to work for good. Anger's force can provide the get-up-and-go we need to stop being apathetic and instead fully engage with life. Because the feeling itself is not a sin and because anger truly has benefits, it's time to pay attention to its work in our hearts and our lives. Taking the assessment[2] and then plowing through the chapter may take some courage, friends. So let's go to it.

An emotion itself is neither good nor bad. It's how we act upon it that determines its effect in our life.

ANGER ASSESSMENT

*Remember, the less you think after reading each statement, the better.
Just answer honestly—these statements are for you alone but will help
immensely as you continue reading the chapter. Please choose "mostly
true" or "mostly false" for your answer.*

1. In the past month, I've spoken or acted in anger in a way that I
   immediately regretted.
   ____ mostly true   ____ mostly false

2. If I'm in a situation where I feel I was wronged, I am most likely to go
   to someone other than the person who offended me to vent my
   frustrations.
   ____ mostly true   ____ mostly false

3. I sometimes use sarcasm to make a point.
   ____ mostly true   ____ mostly false

4. When I see people or creation mistreated, I get angry and want to do
   something to make things right.
   ____ mostly true   ____ mostly false

5. I have taken out my anger on an undeserving person.
   ____ mostly true   ____ mostly false

6. In the past month, I have screamed, hit something, or thrown
   something in anger.
   ____ mostly true   ____ mostly false

7. When something makes me angry, I tend to replay it in my head
   repeatedly.
   ____ mostly true   ____ mostly false

8. It's hard for me to express myself to a person who has made me angry.
   ____ mostly true   ____ mostly false

9. I have taken specific action to combat injustice in this world.
   ____ mostly true   ____ mostly false

10. I have a cause (e.g., slavery, orphans, famine) that I have educated
    myself about and financially contribute to.
    ____ mostly true   ____ mostly false

11. I'm more likely to bear a grudge than to have an outright conflict with
    someone who has wronged me.
    ____ mostly true   ____ mostly false

A QUICK BODY LESSON

In college I enrolled in a class called Adventure Games. I have no idea what the syllabus actually claimed, but the class could have been subtitled "Ways to produce an adrenaline rush." Every Thursday morning we showed up for a different risk-taking venture. We Australian rappelled (facing forward) off the football stadium, climbed rocks, and swung from ropes high in the pine trees surrounding campus.

Adventure Games induced the self-created high known as an adrenaline rush, which hones all of your senses to focus on the present moment. It primes your muscles for action. Your heart rate goes up and oxygen rushes to your lungs to prepare you for activity. Extra sugar is released into your muscles for energy. No wonder we call it a "rush"!

The emotion of anger triggers a similar physiological response. The very same chemical that's involved in an adrenaline rush is released when the brain sends out the "anger alarm" to the body. If you've ever experienced such anger, you know that it's a powerful, strong emotion. Your body's response to anger is a heightened physical intensity, one that would prepare you for a physical fight or help you get away. This is known as the fight-or-flight response.

However, last I checked, my daughter misplacing her hand grip was not an actual life-or-death circumstance. Herein lies the issue: most of the time, this "physical supercharge"[3] is unnecessary and can actually hinder our healthy response to anger. But it's an important detail to consider as we evaluate our own ways of managing this force.

Our bodies' response to feelings of anger—no matter what the cause—is the same. Yet, according to author Richard Walters, anger is expressed in three distinct ways, each of which produces very different results. The first two expressions, rage and resentment, are destructive ways to deal with anger. The third, indignation, is a "constructive, loving expression."

Rage

If you answered "mostly true" to statements 1, 5, or 6, you have used rage as an outlet for anger. Let's use my example of the loss of Cameron's hand grip to evaluate one way anger shows up in our lives. Before we sat down for breakfast, Cameron and I realized the grips could not be found. As I checked every room of the house, a silent power began to build in my brain. At a mental crossroads, I had multiple voices to listen to. The voice of reason was quiet and reassuring. *This really isn't a big deal, Nicole. You lose things all of the time. Keep calm.* The voice of anger was louder, more insistent, and less rational. *This is such a pain! I don't have time for this! She always loses things! I told her ten times not to touch those hand grips! I'm going to be late for work.* On this morning, I'm ashamed (a by-product of rage) to admit that I took the well-traveled path, allowing the thoughts of anger to walk me further and further toward rage. After several minutes, my emotions had clearly tripped my brain into action and I felt the all-too-familiar adrenaline rush of anger building.

The physiological trigger of anger has to be reconciled. Anger always needs a vent.

My inner thoughts came out, and I actually started muttering to myself as I stomped around the kitchen (um, yes, crazy lady alert). And then, in typical anger mode, I couldn't take it anymore. I slammed the empty hand-grip bag down on the counter and took a deep breath to scream up the steps, "I told you not to touch those grips!" At just that moment, however, my babysitter walked through the front door. I caught the scream at the roof of my mouth and swallowed it away.

I'm ashamed again to admit that it was only her presence

that kept me from screaming up the steps. I had hurtled myself down the path of anger, and the only way to return to normal was to vent that anger. My chosen method was screaming, and yet I was stymied—not by my desire to love my daughter well, not by my ability to practice self-control, not by my patience— but by the presence of someone else walking into my house that morning.

Lashing out is a great way to release that powerful emotion— because it works! Like the calm that follows a severe storm, our bodies often return to a peaceful state after we erupt. But, oh, the destruction our rage leaves behind! Not only can we create permanent damage to the object of our anger—whether through violent actions or words—but we also create permanent damage in our own hearts. That's because anger often leads to another powerful emotion—shame.

Shame is the product of anger released in rage. Most of us are shocked by the force within us and our ability to lash out with such hatred. We immediately try to cover ourselves, hiding behind justifications for our actions and listing a litany of reasons why we responded that way. Some of us stay there, allowing our justifications to keep us blind to the damage we are causing to others. But I believe that anyone who takes the time to evaluate the moments they've reacted in rage or anger is not comfortable with their response. Most of the time, we hate ourselves for it. We survey the damage, and we are embarrassed and pained. And if we do not have an intervention with the Lord, we become angry at ourselves. The buildup of shame covered by anger primes the physiological pump for yet another episode.

Friends, we cannot condemn ourselves for the feeling of anger itself, nor for our response to it. Rather, when we courageously

Shame is the product of anger released in rage.

look at the truth of ourselves within it, we can begin the process of relearning a proper response to the emotion.

Resentment

If you answered "mostly true" to statements 2, 3, 7, 8, or 11, you may vent your anger through resentment. If so, the following image might be helpful: Picture the emotion of anger as a beach ball. Our soul is the pool, and the beach ball of anger sometimes lands on its surface. In order to maintain balance in our souls, we must deal with the beach ball. We can either punt it out of the pool (rage) or press it under the surface of the water (resentment). Just like a beach ball, resentment must constantly be pushed down to keep it under the surface. The second we take our attention from it, it tends to pop back up. Sarcasm directed toward other people, grudges, and unresolved conflict are all expressions of resentment. We can also respond in a passive-aggressive manner when we get angry, choosing to "not act" as a method of getting our way or making our point.

To return to the "morning of the lost hand grip" example, let's rewind my actions and see what the response might have been if I had taken that anger and swallowed it down without giving it an appropriate vent. Let's imagine that I give up looking for the grips. I kiss Cameron good-bye and, because I see worry in her eyes, I tell her, "Of course, sweetie, it's fine that you lost your grips." I smile but roll my eyes as I turn away.

Meanwhile, all that simmering, swirling force of emotion is still inside of me. I tell myself once or twice to let it go, but throughout the day I find myself returning to the situation, playing it over in my head. Instead of the path of rage, I trip down the path of resentment.

That night at dinner, I ask Cameron about her day at gymnastics. I make a joke, "Good thing your head is screwed on or you might lose it like your grips!" When I send her to bed, I remark to my husband while she's still in earshot, "I hope Cami doesn't get lost on her way to bed. I wouldn't want to lose her like she lost her hand grip. Good thing I'm more careful with my things!"

When she finally goes to bed, I gripe to Dave about what happened that morning. Instead of feeling relieved, I feel even more resentful, strangely enough. I find myself replaying all the ways that the family disrespects my authority and never listens to anything I say.

Although I haven't spoken out in anger, something equally poisonous is happening—only it's inside me, where that powerful emotion of anger is now simmering. And like a sauce bubbling on the stove, my anger is intensifying, turning into a potent force within me called bitterness. Resentment is the monster of rage disguised in pretty clothes.

Women who condemn the emotion of anger itself immediately suppress it without listening to what it's telling them. Yet that beach ball of resentment requires so much emotional energy that these women usually miss out on really enjoying life. And it's not just rage that can create scars, resentment can as well. It is an insidious force that ruins relationships, our enjoyment of life, and our ability to love. Resentment is closely related to the issue of control and often causes us to act out in manipulative ways. Because we haven't learned to deal directly with our anger, this monster begins to control us.

> *Resentment is the monster of rage disguised in pretty clothes.*

Because I've been dealing with my issues for a while, I have almost as many stories of triumph as I do of failure. I am pleased when I think of how God is refining me, even though lost hand grips and my own failures often get the best of me. But more than anything, I take heart in knowing that when I let God in on even my ugliest sin, he can change my actions and actually turn that same passionate predisposition into a force that can be used for good.

Indignation, a.k.a. righteous anger

If you answered "mostly true" to statements 4, 9, and 10, you've experienced the power of anger used for good. Of course, it's tempting to assume that many of our reactions come out of righteous anger. The term itself leads us to assume it describes "my anger when I'm right." And with that definition, it's easy to explain almost all anger. I'm angry and *right* when someone crosses the white line and cuts me off. I'm angry and *right* when my husband doesn't do what he told me he would. And I'm angry and *right* when Cameron loses her hand grip even after I reminded her to keep them in their bag. Well, no. Righteous anger doesn't have anything to do with us being "right." Very few of us get mad without reason. We do have a reason . . . but it often is expressed far beyond what the situation warrants and causes more damage than the original sin!

Scripture, however, enables us to determine exactly how God models righteous indignation. When Jesus became indignant in the Gospels, it was directed at real evil in the world. When Jesus was angry at the Pharisees in Mark 3:5, he "grieved [because of] the hardness of their hearts" (NKJV). When Jesus was angry and threw the money changers out of the Temple in Matthew 21, he was responding to the corruption of the religious class that obstructed "commoners" from coming to worship. When Jesus got mad at his disciples, it was because they were blocking children from getting close to him (see Mark 10:13-14). Every time Scripture describes Jesus as being angry, it was for a real evil that kept people from experiencing God's Kingdom.

In Jesus' declaration of his ministry, which is found in Luke 4:18-19, he spoke of coming to release captives and set the oppressed free. What's the logical reaction, then, to seeing people in bondage? Anger.

Releasing captives and freeing the oppressed is not a cerebral business. Getting involved in the work of Christ requires heart, passion—emotion. And the emotion we feel, at least at first, is often a sense of anger at a true injustice that is being committed.

All the reasons I get angry when I'm "right" fail to measure up to this standard. If I look even more deeply into the anger that comes when I'm "right" versus true righteous anger, I will see that the fruit of the anger will be very different. My own anger produces very bitter fruit. I am ashamed of my actions, and I've used the emotion to destroy something. I've used words that wound, I've physically lashed out, or I've turned my anger into a deep guilt and hatred toward myself.

Righteous indignation produces fruit of a different kind. Indignation creates words and actions that heal. It can lead to loving confrontation for the purposes of building others up. The fruit of this anger is sweet and contributes to positive changes within our homes and our communities—even the world. This very emotion can actually bring about a 1 Corinthians 13 love experience. Although passionate, it can also persevere, hope, and never fail. In the hands of the Master, this anger can be a force for love and for good in a world stained and broken by evil.

Author Richard P. Walters notes, "Among Christians there is a fear of rage, a surplus of resentment, and a shortage of indignation."[4] I believe that among women, this is even more true. How often do we frighten ourselves with the power of anger, stuffing it back inside ourselves! How often do we get overly angry about little injustices in our life while turning a blind eye to the tragic injustice all around us! Perhaps we all need a reality check—to gain more self-control when it comes to the daily woes of our lives and a little less control about the things that make God angry.

SPACE BAR

A PRAYER

Father, this emotion business is tricky! And anger is an area that makes me uncomfortable. How to express it? When to express it, and with whom? Thank you, my Father God, for the promise that when we turn to you, you wipe away our sins and refresh us (Acts 3:19). Refresh me for the work of sorting through my anger. Amen.

A JOURNALING EXERCISE

When was the last time you were angry? Journal or devote some time to thinking about it. Who were you angry with? Why were you angry? What were the circumstances? Was the situation reconciled? Are you likely to over- or underreact to anger? This exercise will give you a fresh memory with which to read the next chapter, so try to sort through as many details as possible.

_____

_____

_____

_____

_____

FOR GROUP DISCUSSION

1. Review your anger assessment. Are you more likely to be full of rage or resentful? How does that response manifest itself in your life?

2. What are some of the ways you justify the actions that stem from anger? Do you find yourself apologizing because you are tired, stressed out, etc.?

3. Was anger expressed in your house as you were growing up? Was it a positive or negative experience for you?

Hear from Nicole why anger has such power—and what it means about what's happening in your life. Snap the code with your smartphone or visit the link below.

www.tyndal.es/ShesGotIssues11

CHAPTER 12

HOW TO CHANGE A WICKED WITCH

*Anyone can become angry—that is easy, but to be angry with
the right person at the right time, and for the right purpose and in
the right way—that is not within everyone's power and that is not easy.*

ARISTOTLE

THE TENSION IN THE ROOM was almost palpable. I had cut the counseling session short, speaking over the din. "I cannot allow you to continue to speak in this way," I said firmly to the woman sitting across from me in my office. It was the only family counseling session I'd ever had that I thought might end in a walkout, a shouting match, or actual punches.

My office was full; three teenage children plus mom and dad had us all crowded together, knees almost touching. The session had started normally enough. There had been some laughter but that had faded as soon as I began asking the parents some questions. My client was the teenage daughter, but two weeks into our counseling relationship, I had realized there was much more going on. Allegations of abuse—both verbal and physical—had emerged.

I had talked with each family member separately, and now we had come together to attempt to unravel the mess and make some progress forward. After the formalities, the father, in a surprisingly mild-mannered tone, stepped his toe into the ring with these words to his wife, "Sometimes I think you might be too harsh with the kids." As I pressed him further, he brought up a recent incident when his wife had pulled her teenage daughter's hair.

His wife's smiling face (frozen in place since the beginning of the session) twisted into an angry sneer. A torrent of words poured forth. With painted fingernail stabbing the air, the wife began to bring down her husband, attacking his parenting style, his ability to love her, his manliness. She raised her thin frame off the couch as she detailed long-standing resentments, some from over ten years before. I half-expected her to take off her stiletto and beat him with it. Occasionally one of the kids would chime in, trying hard to protect their father from the barrage. Meanwhile, he sat so still and silent that I knew this wasn't a new experience. When the wife began to mock a conversation between her husband and his mother, actually imitating their voices, I called a halt to the session.

It was a debacle.

We were sitting in a very pleasant office in a pleasant part of town. This was a family that from all outward appearances were good Christian people. Yet the vitriol and hate that spewed in that room was enough to melt the plastic leaves off my ficus tree!

How does this happen? How do two people who profess to know and love God, who clearly started off in a loving relationship, end up here? And more important for our purposes, how does a beautiful woman full of life and vigor turn into the Wicked Witch of the West End of Richmond?

I don't tell you this story so you can think to yourself, *At least I'm not like that!* Truly, this woman screamed things many women have thought. She was the power of anger in motion. My guess is she didn't remember half of what she said once anger had taken over and ruled her tongue. One reason anger is so deadly is because of the way it controls our speech.

Remember the discussion back in chapter 1 about the "new commandment" Jesus introduced? It's easy to see that the rage and resentment that rise from our anger demonstrate the opposite of love. We cannot experience both anger and love at the same time. One crowds out the other, which may be why Paul admonishes us, "Don't let the sun go down while you are still angry" (Ephesians 4:26). Once anger takes root, it chokes out love.

Perhaps this is also why parents who are angry can do such damage. I have often wondered how many of the words I've spoken in anger will be remembered by my children—and whether those words might outweigh the ones spoken in love.

Think back on your own life. If you're like most people, you have a memory seared into your brain of a time when someone said harmful words to you. Hopefully, you have also experienced great words of encouragement and healing; the sad truth is that we usually need those words to help us heal from other ugly words.

WHY AM I ANGRY?

Think about the last time you were angry. There are a myriad of reasons you might list, such as:

- being disrespected
- feeling misunderstood
- hearing someone question your character
- feeling out of control
- wanting something to go your way and it didn't
- feeling frustrated
- being treated unfairly
- being self-focused due to physical or emotional pain

Can you name more?

You may notice a sobering reality: almost every reason we get angry has to do with ourselves. Our impatience. Our agenda. Our control. Our idea of how things should go. It is rare to experience an occasion for anger that is other-centered.

"In facing up to our anger," says Jerry Bridges, "we need to realize that no one else *causes* us to be angry."[1] That truth caught me off guard. It cuts deep to say my anger is *never* caused by someone else. Now, you want to yell at me: "Nicole, you are *not* married to my husband, and you don't have to relate to my mother-in-law. If you had to deal with them, you would be angry too!"

Let me liberate you now! If you are an adult who is not in an abusive relationship, is not living life under a burka in Pakistan, or is not being held as a slave in India, then you actually don't have anyone controlling you! What if you and I decided to strike forever from our vocabulary, "He [or she or they] made me do it"? This is a wonderfully freeing and shocking reality. It's freeing because once we grasp this truth, we will suddenly feel unchained from other people and their actions. It's shocking because it means we have to take control of our own behavior.

One of the greatest myths of our womanhood is that other people "make" us lash out in anger.

Remember the story about Cameron's hand grips? It's obvious Cameron didn't *make* me get angry. I *chose* to respond to that situation in anger. But whether it's my husband's criticism or my coworker's slander or another driver's rude behavior, the way I respond to him is *my choice*. And because it's *my choice*, I am completely responsible for my actions. Of course, things will happen and people will act and speak in ways that bring on anger, that tempt me to act in anger, that I have anger about. But the choice to respond *in* anger is actually mine.

Oh, how these words would bring me to tears just a few years ago. The fact that my hyenalike anger was caused by me alone makes me cry just thinking about it. Do you feel inadequate? At the end of your rope? Do you feel like you can't stand to live with the woman you are becoming or have been? Take heart, friend! This is exactly where God will meet you. In fact, Jesus has something to say to you in your beaten-down, dragged-out reality.

WORD UP

Just like the issue of control, anger can illuminate the truth of our own poverty of spirit. Remember the ridiculous truth that Jesus declared: "Blessed are the poor in spirit, for theirs is the kingdom of heaven" (Matthew 5:3, NIV). Commentators point out that the Greek rendering for *theirs* implies exclusivity, meaning, "Blessed are the poor in spirit, for theirs *and only theirs* is the kingdom of heaven."

Jesus tells us exactly how we can experience God's heavenly Kingdom right here and now. When we recognize our own deficits and inability to control our issues, we are able to embrace the true reality of God's grace.

What does it mean to be poor in spirit? It means coming to the end of yourself and realizing you are lacking—lacking love, lacking patience, lacking the energy to act like you've got it together. It means recognizing the ugly side of yourself (anger will do that for you). It's here—and only here—that you can experience the true power of Jesus' transforming power in your life. It's here—and only here—that you can embrace the strength of the Spirit moving and working within you.

We can try to prevent anger (we'll talk about that next). We can employ techniques to diffuse anger (we'll cover that, too). But the most important thing we can do when anger rises and we are at the crossroads of rage and resentment is to ask God to stand there with us. We can actually invite him into that ugliness.

One of my favorite promises in Scripture is this: "Whether you turn to the right or to the left, your ears will hear a voice behind you, saying, 'This is the way; walk in it'" (Isaiah 30:21, NIV). What an incredible truth this is! As I stand at the mental crossroad of raging or suppressing my anger, I can invite God to be in that place with me, and he will tell me how to walk. I can be assured that God will provide a way out from my anger that doesn't involve screaming or sarcasm. God can replace my anger with spirit-born love.

Julie Barnhill talks about the way she learned to ask God into this moment after many failures to control her anger:

> Unlike in those early she's-gonna-blow years . . . this time
> I decided to ask God immediately (almost) for help. So
> this is what I prayed . . . *please help me hear differently and*
> *change my heart toward [my children]*. . . . When God gets
> involved in the solution, He always, always, always softens
> our hearts with love.[2]

Julie experienced God's transformation by surrendering to the truth that she had issues and that she couldn't change them—only God could! As a result, she experienced a change in perspective and a softened heart. Her children had a less angry, more loving mom. I think the story Julie tells is a Kingdom-of-Heaven kind of story. When Julie realized how desperately she needed God in the here and now, the everyday drudgery of life, she experienced something totally new. And that happens only when we recognize how "poor in spirit" we truly are!

So what then? Our own bitterness, the way we yell, the feelings we harbor toward others—these are the sins that remind us of our desperate need for God. But the "poor in spirit" verse isn't a free pass to stop trying or to wash our hands of all responsibility.

Rather, Scripture tells us that "since we live by the Spirit, let us keep in step with the Spirit" (Galatians 5:25, NIV). Jesus says the person who "listens to my teaching and obeys me is wise, like a person who builds a house on solid rock" (Matthew 7:24). Notice that in these verses God is present and moving while we are keeping in step and building. And when it comes to responding differently in situations that make us turn into wild hyenas, we have to get to work.

PREVENTATIVE MEASURES

In the last chapter you were invited to uncover your own tendencies to respond to the emotion of anger with resentment or rage. Now I encourage you to think about what triggers you to respond in that way. Think back to the last time you lost your temper or felt resentment toward someone. Often you and I justify our bad behavior with a litany of reasons why we lost it. We were tired. We were stressed out. We had a headache. We hadn't yet reconciled after our last argument. We were preoccupied with other emotional stress. In fact, it can be helpful to step back and list what mental, physical, or emotional conditions are likely to predispose us to losing it.

One of my favorite activities when staying at the home of friends or family members is to peruse the homeowner's book collection. On one trip to the beach I picked up an old, mildewed textbook entitled *Home Economics*, eager to discover just what future housewives in the 1950s were learning about their chosen "career." The book contained a line graph depicting the supply/demand of the family life cycle. As you can imagine, the woman's "supply" of energy remained mostly steady with a slight decline as she aged.

The other line depicted the "demand" of the family. If you have ever watched a toddler for more than five minutes, you know the demands of raising young children far exceed the mother's time, ability, and "supply."

That line graph, while not really telling me anything I didn't know, was like a portal of time travel for my weary soul. I imagined my mother, my grandmother, and her mother each holding a book like this, looking for tools for living, ways to understand the seasons of her life to come. My guess is that each one of them, like me, had no idea what it would actually be like to live in a constant state of near-drowning in demands, dishes, and diapers. They probably didn't know that their reality would result in a lack of patience, a lack of love, and a new, distressing reality of what it means to be "poor in spirit." As I flipped through the book, I also recognized that if I were going to live in the constant tension of never having enough time to feel like I had met all the demands on me, I'd better take my own emotional health seriously.

One rainy, dreary Saturday a few months after flipping through that textbook, I came up with a brief list of the preventative techniques I needed to take to keep my emotional health stable. My statement was so pithy that one of my author friends put it in her book.[3] All I needed, I said, was to run, read, and rest—take a nap in the course of a weekend—and my heart would be restored. This is all true. I had discovered what preventative measures keep me balanced and able to handle the tsunami of demands that raising young children brings.

Do you have a sense of what proactive measures keep you primed to handle your emotions? Do you have a sense of what it means to live a relatively healthy life: in your food choices, in exercise, in solitude, or in activities that feed your brain? Do you pay attention to your hormonal cycles, the amount of sleep you get? Do you pay attention to the signals your body sends that it's time to slow down? Are you able to say no to people and things when you need to recharge?

My pithy "three-R" restoration plan was all well and good. For a while. But there came a time where there was always (I mean *always*) a household emergency, no matter what time I laced up my running shoes. On some days my eyes were so bleary that even reading *Curious George* to my toddler felt like a challenging feat. Sleeping, I decided, was a luxury afforded only women not of childbearing years. When my three Rs failed, I had the occasional mommy meltdown via text message with my husband. Our exchange usually went something like this:

Me: I'm dying over here.

Him: Why?

Me: I can't stop crying. I just want to go to sleep. I can't take it anymore. My life is over.

Him: Wow, I just wish you would tell me how you really feel.

Me: Don't make me come down there. Actually, no, please do make me come down there. I have to get out of this house.

Him: I'll be home by six.

Me: Hopefully everyone will still be alive.

My husband became my hero when he sent me out for the evening alone or with a friend, or when he simply sent me to bed. These are the kind of preventative measures that we need to have in place. Ladies, it is not wrong to take time for ourselves. The old slogan "When mama's not happy, ain't nobody happy" couldn't be more true. We need to recognize the healthy outlets we have to release our tension and anger, and then we must get honest with ourselves before God about the reasons for our anger.

BUT I'M ALREADY TRIGGERED!

I hope you are beginning to think about what measures you can put into place to create space for emotional balance. I have an awesome twentysomething friend who's learning to find her own balance. Because she's struggled with depression in the past, whenever she feels particularly irritated, she fears she'll land in another episode of depression.

On one of her emotionally stormy days recently, we shared a pot of tea and a heart-to-heart chat. She shared her woes, and then I asked, "I'm not your mom, but what time did you go to bed last night?"

"Two a.m.," she responded forlornly, staring into her tea.

"Okay, once again I acknowledge I'm not your mom, but when did you get your last period?"

"Um," she thought for a moment, "I guess it's been about a month."

"All right," I said, smiling. "Do you think that maybe this storm will pass, that your life isn't in fact almost over, and that you probably can ride out these blues for a couple of days and then reevaluate how you are really doing?"

She agreed. Turns out, the mom in me was right. She wasn't about to fall off the cliff into the abyss of depression. She just needed a good night's sleep and a Midol.

There are times when we overreact to our emotional situations, but there are other times when we underreact. My three-R "balance" plan worked for a while, but there was a period when nothing seemed to work. I kept insisting I just needed to go for a run, just needed a night off, just needed to sleep—but nothing seemed to keep me from becoming an irritable mess no one wanted to be around. After I screamed for the third time before lunch for the third time that week, I put myself in time-out. I flipped on the TV for the kids and proceeded to my walk-in closet.

My closet became my sanctuary in that angry moment. Between the shoes and bags cluttering the floor, there was just enough room for me to lie all the way down. I closed the door on myself and lay in the darkness. The sounds of the day were muffled enough for me to focus my attention inward and upward, although I was so ashamed of my actions that I wouldn't dare show my face to God. Like the woman caught in adultery lying at Jesus' feet, I preferred to inhale the carpet fibers rather than actually imagine God seeing and knowing my every thought and action.

When you feel anger rising, apply some mom-wisdom and put yourself in time-out. Take a walk, take a break in your car, or hide in the closet.

Face hidden, I confessed the bitterness and anger in my heart that had scared me. I had been in this place long enough to know that this anger wasn't just about young children. It was a more deeply rooted anger and frustration borne from living a life I wasn't willing to accept. It was a prideful spirit that didn't want to bow to God's plan and timing. It was a selfish root that wanted things to go just my way.

In that dark space, I recognized that I had no choice but to surrender—again—to God's way and to come to him for my needs. I was like Peter, who knew he had no choice but to follow Jesus, even when times got tough.

We encounter one such poignant moment between Jesus and his disciples in John 6. Jesus has just performed yet another miracle of provision—feeding the hungry thousands who now follow him, craning their necks to catch the next miracle from this unlikely Savior. As the miracle meal is still digesting in their bellies, Jesus hits the crowd with a difficult teaching on "eating his flesh" and "drinking his blood," referring to what it means to have Christ dwell within them. As you can imagine, this kind of teaching didn't go over that well, and Scripture says "at this point many of his disciples turned away and deserted him" (John 6:66).

Jesus turns to Peter and his band of friends and asks, "Will you leave me too?" Take that in with me for a second. Jesus—the perfect one. Jesus—who bears all of our burdens. Jesus—whose love took him to the Cross for us. Jesus says to his disciples and to us, "Times are tough. Are you going to leave me?"

When anger prevails in your heart; when life isn't turning out the way you expect; when conflict with your friend or husband or boss is so much more painful than you ever imagined—it is at such crossroads that many decide to turn their backs on Jesus. Their salvation-ticket theology fails them. They realize that following Christ is truly a narrow path fraught with difficulties. And Jesus isn't a stone statue, unaffected by these storms. He turns to us and asks, "You aren't going to leave me now, are you?"

If you've closed your heart to Jesus because of your anger, I want you to imagine him asking you if you are leaving him. He is grieved by your absence. He wants to know if you will come to him in your strength as well as your weakness. He wants to know if you will come to him even when you have to wait for an answer, when you are living in a relationship that seems beyond repair, or when your own shame smothers you. He wants to know if you will continue to follow him even when the path seems dim and your steps unsure.

Peter stands before Jesus with a choice. Will he go or will he stay? Peter responds to Jesus' question with this: "Lord, to whom would we go? You alone have the words that give eternal life" (see John 6:68). What a moment! How often have I felt trapped between what I want God to be for me and my own stubborn way of living. But nothing like my face-down closet moment has brought me closer to the rock-bottom reality that nothing—not rest, not reading, not a girl's night, not anything—can bring peace to my soul like Jesus' words. It wasn't a three-mile run or a coffee date with a friend or a great book that diffused my deep-seated anger. It was a holy moment in a closet.

In my poverty of spirit, in the midst of my anger, God was sufficient. And every time I lie on the floor before him, I'm reminded again that he is real. That he does supply my every need, that he hears me when I call.

BUT WHAT ABOUT MY #&%* MOUTH?

"Speak when you are angry and you'll make the best speech you'll ever regret."[4] We've all received the blow of hurtful words as well as thrown such a punch ourselves. Words are a vent for anger, and they seem less damaging than physically lashing out or manipulating others. But unfortunately they can cause great destruction. James 3:5 says, "The tongue is a small thing, but what enormous damage it can do. A tiny spark can set a great forest on fire."

Once when my husband, Dave, and I were dating, he said an incredibly hurtful thing to me. It was over fifteen years ago, and I still remember the exact moment he said it, the tone of his voice, the words he chose. The image and the words are burned in my brain. Although I've long since forgiven him, the memory remains.

We must take our words seriously. Once they are sent out, they cannot be taken back. We often immediately regret words spoken in anger—they spark within us and cause enormous damage, like the blaze of a forest fire that causes years of growth to be burned to the ground.

Whew, I feel convicted just writing that and so concerned that I watch my words so they don't wreck someone's life! Thank our sweet Lord that he is bigger than our words and can heal even when we wound. Otherwise, I might have to commit myself to life as a mime! If you feel deeply convicted like I do, don't let a spirit of condemnation overwhelm you. Instead, allow the godly sorrow of sin to move you toward repentance and salvation, which leaves no regret at all (see 2 Corinthians 7:10). We move forward in the strength of what we've learned so far: that God will help us, if we let him.

Let's take the command of Ephesians 4:29 as a starting point for our transformed speech: "Do not let any unwholesome talk come out of your mouths, but only what is helpful for building others up according to their needs, that it may benefit those who listen" (NIV). This verse gives us a practical road map for choosing what to say and how to say it:

Our talk shouldn't be "unwholesome." The Greek word used in the original manuscript is *sapros*, which means rotten, decayed, corrupted, useless, or unfit for use. Here's a quick method of evaluating our words: Are they rotten? Are they corrupt? Do we use double entendres or sly remarks? Perhaps even more relevant: Are our words useless? What is the intended result of our stories, our advice, our questions, our chatter?

Our words should be used to build others up. They should be helpful and benefit the listener. This is a high call! If every word we spoke were recorded for a day so we could review them, how many of them would build others up? How many of them would be spoken to benefit the listener, not draw attention to ourselves? How many would be about their needs and not our own agendas?

Our words should be used "according to [the receiver's] needs." This speaks to the timing of our words. So often we women have good, helpful thoughts, but we fail to determine the best time to speak them! We act on impulse rather than obedience.

There is nothing like a little time to confirm exactly what your words are intended to do. Let's say you have a pressing piece of advice you'd like to give a friend, yet your schedules have conflicted and you haven't been able to get together. Sometimes time is the gift that helps God refine your own agenda in your words. And if those words are in fact from the Lord, you better believe he will hound you relentlessly until you share them!

We pay attention to our words because they are a thermometer to our hearts. Jesus said "Whatever is in your heart determines what you say" (Matthew 12:34). When our hearts are right with God, we naturally reflect that in the way we speak. We find ourselves living out of love. Encouraging our family members, coworkers, even strangers. We can't help but share the love we have. And when things aren't so good? The words that spill forth from this place are often the first sign of a true heart sickness.

"BUT I'M ANGRY ALL THE TIME"

Erin was one of those clients who presented herself as if we had just gathered for a Starbucks date. We exchanged pleasantries as she settled into my office, and I waited expectantly for her to tell me why she had come to counseling. Minutes ticked by as she skirted around the issue, instead asking me about ministry, my children's photos, and my shoes. She spent a while telling me about her life, all of which sounded very pleasant. It wasn't until almost the end of the session that she ran out of nice things to say, and we sat in silence while she examined her manicure.

I started again, "I'd love to know why you made this appointment, Erin." She turned her eyes from her fingers to the ceiling, and I noticed her hands clench into fists. Suddenly the words tumbled out. "I've never told anyone this before. But I'm so mad that my husband lost his job and doesn't seem to be doing anything to get another one. I'm so mad that we might lose our house and that we are actually eating into *my* savings to keep us afloat. I'm so [expletive] mad that I have to work when I want to stay home with our kids! I screamed in the shower the other day. I just stood there and let out this huge scream. I feel so angry. I want to leave him; I just want to pack the kids up and get out of this town."

It was Erin's scream in the shower that had prompted her to call for an appointment. She couldn't act like she had it all together anymore when she didn't. The real pressures of life—her husband's job loss, expensive kids' activities, her work schedule—had pushed her over the brink, and now all she felt was a seething, raw rage that threatened to destroy the memory of the last decade of happiness with her husband.

When anger builds—when resentments turn to bitterness, when conflicts turn to war, when everything you've wanted and believed to be your "right" in life crumbles—you may cross over to a serious place of doubt and oppression, a danger zone where it becomes difficult to make logical choices. This kind of anger takes no prisoners and has the power to create generations of grief. Although beyond the scope of this book, there are a couple of things worth mentioning about this type of anger:

1. **A constant undercurrent of anger often covers a more vulnerable feeling.** That emotion might be hurt, rejection, betrayal, or self-hate. You might complete this sentence when you feel this kind of anger: "I am angry *and* [hurt, shamed, disrespected, embarrassed]." This will help you get closer to the root of the issue.

2. **Depression can manifest itself as unrelenting anger.** As mentioned earlier, sometimes depression is anger turned inward. Depression can show up as excessive irritability or restlessness, along with increased feelings of guilt and a general lack of interest in things that used to be enjoyable.

The "blues" or the anger discussed in this chapter can turn into a persistent issue that significantly impairs your school, work, or relationships. If this describes you, please seek out a pastor, medical professional, or counselor. There is help. Check out the resource list at the back of this book.

3. **This kind of persistent anger is often related to unresolved conflict.** The next section on unforgiveness will address the why and how of forgiveness.

THERE IS HOPE

I am thankful that I saw progress with the family I described at the start of this chapter. After calling a halt to our session, I escorted the children to the waiting room and returned to speak with the parents. This time-out allowed heads to cool and rational thought to return. I have never felt so angry at anger as I did in that moment. My anger wasn't directed toward the woman but toward the harm that was falling on these children. It was as if the chains binding this woman were visible, and watching her unleash pain and rage that would surely enslave her own children made me mad. This is the kind of "mad" that rages against sin and fights for love.

This is the kind of "mad" that author Jen Hatmaker addresses in a post on her website. After waiting months to finally meet her adoptive children, she was discouraged and angry by the corrupt government system that was failing her family. Many well-meaning Christians chastised her to maintain a brave face while she waited for her adoptive children to be delivered from their abusive, oppressive situation:

> We are not mad at God; we are mad *with* God. We are not fighting against God; we are fighting *alongside* Him. We are not crying because God is failing us; we are crying

out because 170 million children will go to bed tonight with no parents, and we can not stand this injustice one second longer. These are the tears of the heavens that have been shed since the beginning of time for the least and last, the forgotten and forsaken.[5]

Jen's anger at the situation orphans must endure, my anger at the pain in my office, and whatever burns you up about oppression, injustice, and true evil—that is the power God wants to use in you and through you to bring about his purposes in the world. Don't fear that anger; rather, thank God that he is burning his passion within you!

In fact, that moment in my office was a turning point for the family. The parents agreed to seek out their own marriage counselor. The mother and I discussed some preventative measures she could use to diffuse her anger as well as to address her predisposition to use her children as scapegoats for her frustration with her husband. Two months after the episode in my office, there was great improvement. Once the root of her anger had been addressed, the mother's beauty—in her love for her kids, her surrendered spirit toward the Lord, her improving relationship with her husband—reemerged. It was a modern miracle, testifying to God's ability to transform even the bleakest of situations into a show of his glorious grace.

SPACE BAR

A PRAYER

My God, you are my counselor. You see into my places of resentment and even rage, and you still promise to redeem me. Thank you, God, that when I take refuge in you, I am not condemned (Psalm 34:22). I pray that the freedom of your love would spur me on to change. Soften my heart where there is hardness. I need strength to accept your grace that covers my anger. You give me power to hold my tongue, to diffuse my temper, and to love you more than I love being right or justified in my anger. I pray today that I would choose you. Thank you! Amen.

A JOURNALING EXERCISE

Think back to the incident you journaled about in the last chapter. After reading this chapter, do you have any additional insights into that situation? Did you react in a healthy way? If you could go back to that situation, what would you do differently? What measures (if any) can you put into place to react in a healthier way the next time you are angry?

_____

_____

_____

_____

_____

FOR GROUP DISCUSSION

1. Do you feel like the choice whether or not to respond in anger is within your control?

2. What are some of the proactive measures you might take to help you maintain emotional balance?

3. Have you experienced God's strength in the midst of an argument or an episode of anger? How did it affect your attitude?

4. If "words are the thermometer to your heart," what does your speech reveal about your current temperature? In what area mentioned in Ephesians 4:29 do you need to improve: the wholesomeness of your words, the helpfulness of your words, or the timing of your words?

Get tips from Nicole on how to channel your anger productively. Snap the code with your smartphone or visit the link below.

www.tyndal.es/ShesGotIssues12

CHAPTER 13

UNFORGIVENESS: UPROOTING THE BITTER WEED

Genuine forgiveness does not deny anger but faces it head-on.

ALICE DUER MILLER

IF YOU'VE GOT THE KIND OF ANGER we talked about in the last chapter—then you've got issues.

And if you've got those issues, you probably got a two-for-one: not only anger but also its cousin, unforgiveness. Unforgiveness, sown by our wounds, sprouts up like an unwelcome guest and chokes our ability to love, to be compassionate, and to experience freedom. The Miracle-Gro of this unforgiveness comes when we develop a keen sensitivity toward any other wrong directed toward us. If left unchecked, unforgiveness thrives like a fairy-tale bean stalk, exploding in strength, eventually reaching into every emotion, thought, and action.

The act of forgiving isn't easy. The bean stalk of unforgiveness doesn't just die and disappear in a moment. And the longer it's allowed to grow, the more strength and work will be required to remove it. So let's discuss why we need to forgive. From there, we'll talk about three particular aspects of forgiveness: forgiving others, forgiving God, and forgiving ourselves.

Everyone has to pull the weeds of unforgiveness, tending to the daily removal of resentment over slights and tension in order to be free to love. But many of us also know about the bean stalk, the mammoth weed we try to ignore until it kills off almost everything else. I've experienced the damage that harboring bitterness can bring, and I've seen the amazing fruit of allowing God to free us to love with passion, boldness, and strength—all because of forgiveness. If you struggle with unforgiveness, take heart. Becoming free from this issue is evidence that miracles still happen.

WHY FORGIVE?

There's nothing like raising a preschooler to discover what you know—and what you don't know. And my children have always been good at asking hard questions! When our oldest, Charlie, was about five, Dave and I began to notice that his justice meter seemed to operate at a particularly sensitive setting. If a rule was being broken, he knew it. If things didn't seem fair, he appeared on the scene. He would insist on things being made right, from whose turn it was to clear the table to which sibling really didn't brush his or her teeth that morning. When Charlie got going, Dave and I whispered a code sentence: "The sheriff's back in town." We'd serve as a tag team, pulling our little deputy to the side and coaching him through the inevitable wrongs committed in our household.

I'm thankful for Charlie's well-honed sense of justice, because I've grown in my own understanding as I teach him what God really means when he says, "Forgive us our sins, as we forgive others." So let's take a remedial lesson through the reasons we are called to forgive:

We forgive because it's God's way. The first reason we forgive is simple. Scripture makes it quite clear that we are required to forgive. Unfortunately, I think many of us have been taught this as a simple prescription for all of life's problems, as if forgiving someone should come as easily as taking out the trash.

I wonder sometimes about people who teach this. I wonder if they've ever heard a woman's story of persistent and severe sexual abuse at the hands of her father. I wonder if they've ever experienced bullying or slander, or come toe-to-toe with true evil in this world. My guess is that they haven't. Because if they had, they would never treat forgiveness so lightly.

It is important that we understand that God commands us to forgive because without forgiveness there is no love. But although his command is simple and bold, it isn't always easy. If you are one of those people who've been hurt by the simplified, shrug-it-off command to forgive, I would like to say how sorry I am for that. And I humbly ask you to look again at this command, for the true life-giving force it can be in your heart.

I know some friends who can shrug and say, "I forgive easily." I do believe that some personalities and circumstances make it easier for certain people to forgive those who wrong them. But nonetheless, examining our souls for the weeds of unforgiveness is a lifelong process. Often a passive resentment or deadness inside is an indicator that we must look again to make sure we aren't harboring anger toward someone else, ourselves, or even God. Then we must turn our attention to the work of forgiveness if we are to free ourselves for passionate, unbridled love for God and for others.

Forgiveness reflects God's character. The Israelites first heard about forgiveness as an aspect of God's nature. He called himself a "God of forgiveness" (Nehemiah 9:17) and acted on it, showing them mercy again and again as they rebelled against his way. God promises that when his people pray and earnestly seek him he will forgive their sins (see 2 Chronicles 7:14). When the psalm writers confessed their sins, they acknowledged that the unbearable burden of wrongdoing is relieved only through seeking God's forgiveness. Psalm 130:4 says, "With you there is forgiveness" (NIV). Psalm 86:5 says, "You are forgiving and good" (NIV).

If you are lacking in love, you may be lacking in forgiveness.

Forgiveness is the turning point in the story of our eternal lives. I love when science backs up God. (It happens, I promise!) The Mayo Clinic released an article citing the results of numerous studies that examine the effects of holding grudges. People who do so have higher heart rates, higher blood pressure, and more tendencies toward depression.[1] God's command to forgive is backed up by God's design for our bodies and souls. Our Creator knew what he was doing when he spoke boldly in his Word about forgiveness!

Our understanding of forgiveness—developed as we receive it from Christ as well as extend it to others—is the climax of the story of our lives. Forgiveness is the turning point in our testimonies. In God's crazy love, he makes the very place of our deepest hurt the new growth place of our every hope.

Let's examine one more reason why we forgive:

Forgiveness is a tool of the gospel. Jesus makes it clear that forgiveness is a continual process. I don't know about you, but I need God to cleanse me of my own sin and shortcomings every day. We should be ready to forgive others just as frequently.

Jesus hinges our entire relationship with God on forgiveness: "If you forgive those who sin against you, your heavenly Father will forgive you. But if you refuse to forgive others, your Father will not forgive your sins" (Matthew 6:14-15).

At first glance, this command may feel impossible. The justice-seeking part of me protests loudly against this command. My own nature wants to say, like my sheriff son, "That's not *fair!*" Why do other people's wrongs against me have to relate to my wrongs? I want God to be ever merciful, ever patient. I want God to empathize with me when I do wrong, but then I want him to understand why he shouldn't demand that I forgive others for the deep wounds they've caused me. Here we run into a collision of beliefs and the ways we distort God's character for our own purposes. I want God to be merciful toward my sins and just toward others. So which is it?

WORD UP

The disciple Peter wondered about this too. He had hung around Jesus long enough to know that his master seemed really concerned about forgiveness. He had watched Jesus pointedly offer forgiveness of sins to the paralytic, signifying how much more important forgiveness is than any other healing we may experience. Then of course, like adding delicious icing on the cake, Jesus also made his newly forgiven friend able to walk. That's abundance!

So when Peter came to Jesus to ask about forgiveness, he wanted to understand more about Jesus' way of doing the "Kingdom of Heaven." The ethical teaching of that day stressed that if someone wronged you, you should forgive them three times. (This probably stemmed from an interpretation of the book of Amos.[2])

How I love Peter, who was not afraid to put his own spin on the mystery of Jesus! I wonder if he thought to himself, *I know I should forgive. I know Jesus is all about forgiveness. So . . . I'll just multiply three times by two and add one; that's sure to impress him!*

In Matthew 18, we see this play out, as Peter goes to Jesus and asks, "How many times should I forgive my brother? Seven times?"

Jesus responds to Peter with the equation of relentless mercy: "I tell you, not seven times, but seventy-seven times!" Jesus then backs it up with a parable of forgiveness, capturing the concept with such boldness that it's worth reading that passage in its entirety:

> For this reason, the Kingdom of Heaven can be compared to a king who decided to bring his accounts up to date with servants who had borrowed money from him. In the process, one of his debtors was brought in who owed him millions of dollars. He couldn't pay, so the king ordered that he, his wife, his children, and everything he had be sold to pay the debt. But the man fell down before the king and begged him, "Oh, sir, be patient with me, and I will pay it all." Then the king was filled with pity for him, and he released him and forgave his debt.
>
> But when the man left the king, he went to a fellow servant who owed him a few thousand dollars. He grabbed him by the throat and demanded instant payment. His fellow servant fell down before him and begged for a little more time. "Be patient and I will pay it," he pleaded. But his creditor wouldn't wait. He had the man arrested and jailed until the debt could be paid in full.
>
> When some of the other servants saw this, they were very upset. They went to the king and told him what had happened. Then the king called in the man he had forgiven and said, "You evil servant! I forgave you that tremendous debt because you pleaded with me. Shouldn't you have mercy on your fellow servant, just as I had mercy on you?" Then the angry king sent the man to prison until he had paid every penny.
>
> That's what my heavenly Father will do to you if you refuse to forgive your brothers and sisters in your heart.

The story begins with one hard fact: a servant somehow got himself into debt. He went before the king, with whom he did not stand on equal ground. The king acted fairly by saying the man had to pay back what he owed. Like paying a bill, we pay what we owe because it's fair to the lender and to the borrower.

Here we run into the first problem: the servant's debt was so great that there was no way he could ever pay it back. Millions of dollars on a servant's salary while doing jail time? Last I checked, stamping license plates in prison isn't exactly a lucrative business. Yet despite the enormity of the debt and the ridiculousness of the servant's offer to pay it back, the king gives in to his plea and releases him completely from his obligation. The servant doesn't get what he asks for; he gets infinitely *more* than he asks for.

The process of forgiveness begins with our own recognition of the unequal footing we have in the presence of God. We owe God—the giver of breath, the creator of life, the one who sustains us each day and delights us with the abundance of his provision and creation—we owe him everything. Our intelligence, our abilities, our shelter, our paychecks. And this unequal standing exists before we even sin! And sin we do, every day, serving our own interests rather than others. We are in deep debt before God.

When the servant pleaded for mercy, he was given more than he asked for. His debt was forgiven and he was set free. But the servant must have immediately forgotten his own pardon. He went after another servant whose debt against him was almost incalculably smaller than the debt he owed the king. Blinded by his own perverse sense of justice, the forgiven servant gave no mercy to his friend.

Don't overlook the fact that this second servant in the story was also in debt. God doesn't deny the wrongs done to us, but he commands us to view them against the incalculable mercy he has

STUCK IN UNFORGIVENESS?

Consider these options:

1. **Check your heart daily.** Do you have unresolved resentment or tension with loved ones? It takes wisdom to determine what should be confronted and what should be let go. The first step is determining the root of the tension. Does it stem from a deliberate wrong? a misunderstanding? What needs to happen in order for you to feel reconciled to this person?

2. **If you have never resolved an event from your past, write a letter to the person who wounded you (but don't send it).** Think of ways you can "own" parts of the incident for which you had responsibility and also detail how the event has impacted your life. Often the process of writing the letter will help you understand the true impact of the situation and give you clarity about moving forward.

3. **Forgiveness takes time.** The love of others may give you the strength to forgive. Allowing others to see your weaknesses and confessing your bitterness is part of the mysterious process of healing. You were wounded by others—and you may find the most healing when others support and carry you through the process.

4. **Nothing is too small for God.** Perhaps you feel shame that you are still feeling the effects of a middle school bully or a first love's rejection. But there are no petty hurts in God's eyes. The longer you deny their power in your life, regardless of the world's assessment of how big the problems are, the longer the hurt will continue to grow. Deal with your pain, because being enslaved is still slavery, even if the chain seems thin.

given us in the most important relationship of our lives in all of eternity: our relationship with him.

The forgiven servant assumed he could keep his actions against the other servant from the king. Likewise, we can harbor unforgiveness in our hearts, deceiving ourselves into believing that our pain won't harm anyone else. We are blind like this servant, thinking we can maintain that all is well while struggling under the surface with bitterness and resentment. We can try to hide our grudge, but eventually, it affects those around us.

In the servant's first appearance before the king, he was viewed through eyes of mercy. But in his second summons, this servant was called evil. Why the change? Because his heart hadn't reflected the acceptance and fruit of his forgiveness. He had treated the king's mercy with contempt. *Because he demanded justice, he received justice.*

The brutal ending to the story may make us want to turn our anger on the king. But we must not forget that the king was simply treating the first servant as he deserved for his original debt! He did not heap additional punishment on the original debt; out of a sense of justice, he merely required him to repay his debt.

If this story stuns you, it should. If it creates a contrite spirit within you, it should. If it creates some fear in you, it probably should. The fear should not come because of God's wrath but because of God's power to see into your heart, to lay your life before your eyes and ask you to "give an account to God for everything you do" (Ecclesiastes 11:9). If this brings a bad taste to your mouth—when you consider the times you've picked up your own sword and wounded others with your words, with your passivity, or by withholding your love—it should!

Oh friends, we must realize how much we have been forgiven before we can ever begin the difficult journey of forgiving others. Forgiving others is not possible without deep gratitude for the ways we've been forgiven.

"MY BRAIN BELIEVES IT, BUT MY HEART DOESN'T WANT TO ACCEPT IT"

Just because you've now spent a few minutes reflecting on this parable doesn't mean you will immediately be able to forgive those who've deeply wronged you. If you have piled on resentment for months or even years, it is possible to lose it all at once—but it's not probable.

If we piled on thirty pounds over several years of overeating, most of us wouldn't pray and expect God to miraculously bring us back to a normal weight after one jog around the neighborhood! We can pray, though, for the discipline and strength to persevere in making healthy choices.

Unforgiveness is like weight gain. We pile on resentments and hurt, one on top of another. Perhaps we have never let go of one extremely painful situation, and in an attempt to make up for that hurt, we have gorged on many petty resentments along the way. Perhaps we have an underlying resentment about the direction our lives have taken and so feel irritated toward others. Maybe we have never accepted grace for the mistakes we've made and are living under the oppressive burden of our own failures. Regardless of the exact form unforgiveness has taken in our lives, the initial step toward healing is the same.

The first step to losing thirty excess pounds occurs when the overweight person recognizes the problem. In order to stop gaining, he or she must recognize that all, in fact, is not well. The same goes for unforgiveness. The first step is recognizing the problem. The parable of the unmerciful servant shows us our problem—we want mercy for ourselves but justice for others.

Because coming to this realization after suffering great pain can be so difficult, I feel compelled to invite you into the following prayer before we go any further.

Jesus, King of kings, forgiver of sins: I am indebted to you for your sacrifice, which repays my many sins. I can't even comprehend how deeply I've grieved you and how I've hurt others throughout my life. Would you please bring me to a place of understanding my own forgiveness so I can forgive [name person or incident]?

Once we see the connection between God's forgiveness of our sins and our forgiveness of those who've offended us, Scripture hits us with another punch: "If you forgive anyone's sins, they are forgiven. If you do not forgive them, they are not forgiven" (John 20:23). Jesus tells us that once we've accepted the power of his forgiveness in our life, we hold that power within us. The gospel is not just words on paper or an intellectual exercise in belief. The gospel—the good news of Jesus—should be lived out in our lives. The way we forgive others because of the way we've been forgiven is the way we pass on the gospel. When we right our wrongs, when we truly release others from the debt they owe us, we are living examples of the power of the gospel. That power is what compels us to forgive, and that same power is what attracts others to Christ—through us.

Much like the call to healthy living, we are now armed with several reasons why we should choose forgiveness as a way of life. But like healthy living, the doing is much harder than the believing. Most people, Christians or not, believe in the power of forgiveness, but how do we move from forgiveness as a nice ideal to a daily practice? Here are a few places to begin:

1. **Confess your sins.** Apologize with no "buts." Learn to be truly repentant for your own mistakes. Remember that anger may be the right response when we have a reason for it. However, the impulsive or manipulative ways we wound others with our anger are never right.

    Pride and shame may keep you from apologizing for

the ways you've wronged others. I have had to apologize to my children many times for unkind words or actions. It is tempting to say something like, "I'm sorry I yelled about your hand grip, but you should have kept them where I told you." This, my friends, is not an apology. It is not a sincere contrition about the wounds I have inflicted upon my child. It is a justification that I think I'm softening with an apology.

The same is true when it comes to your relationships with other adults. Be on guard, both against keeping your actions passive and hidden so that you never have to admit them and against using all kinds of other niceties to indicate that you're sorry. That is also not an apology. The more aware you are of your own tendencies to sin, to wound, to withdraw love, the more compassionate you will be when those wounds are inflicted on you.

2. **Ask God to give you new eyes.** Maintaining the status quo brings comfort. Even if that status quo is not healthy, at least you understand it. It can become as much a part of your personhood as the color of your hair. When you've held a grudge against someone for a long time, you have generally resigned yourself to the breakdown in that relationship. Making the choice to reexamine that person or event can take more strength than you have.

Ask God to help you see that person with new eyes. Have you ever considered how Jesus sees you? Think about the outcasts and societal "losers" Jesus spent time with. Clearly he didn't judge them by worldly standards. First Samuel 16:7 says, "The LORD does not look at the things man looks at. Man looks at the outward appearance, but the LORD looks at the heart" (NIV).

Don't evaluate through your own eyes those who have

wronged you. Instead, ask God to give you spiritual eyes so that you can see past their wounds and the way they have wounded you and see into their brokenness. This does not excuse their bad behavior, but it can—in a way that only God can do—empower love to win. Your love for them isn't an act of human strength. It is the transformative power of Christ within you that creates love where there is animosity.

I cannot emphasize enough that to forgive doesn't mean to forget. You cannot erase the pains of your past because in doing so you would risk erasing much of yourself. But you can believe that God can transform you and redeem even the most broken of lives.

3. **Recognize that forgiveness is an act of will.** You must not wait until you feel like forgiving. Most of us would be in the grave before our feelings got in line. Instead, see forgiveness as an act of obedience toward your Father God, who so graciously has forgiven you. That may mean asking him to help us extend mercy, perhaps like this: *God, I was so hurt when Amy purposely excluded me this week. I feel angry at her and frustrated because I don't understand what she has against me. But because of your love toward me, I want to let go and grant her forgiveness.*

It has been said that forgiving others is like releasing your grip from their necks. The way they've wounded you creates a desire for revenge, which they justly deserve. But to forgive is to grant mercy, to take your grip off their necks and let them go. When you release others from your grip, you release them into the hands of God. In a great paradox, God is both merciful and just.

The God who knows your heart sees all. Psalm 56:8 says, "Record my lament; list my tears on your scroll—are they not in your record?" (NIV). Your Creator knows every tear you cry. He has seen every wound, every hurt. Your sorrows are not wasted on God. He welcomes your crying out to him, in anger, frustration, sadness, and hurt. When you choose forgiveness, you are not letting anyone off the hook, since judgment isn't in your hands. Choosing forgiveness in the face of evil will bring the strongest force of freedom you will ever experience.

Lewis B. Smedes says, "When we forgive, we set a prisoner free and then discover the prisoner we set free is us."[3] How do you know you've truly extended forgiveness? Smedes says, "You will know that forgiveness has begun when you recall those who hurt you and feel the power to wish them well."[4]

FORGIVING OURSELVES

Psalm 51 was written by King David after he had an affair with Bathsheba and ordered the murder of her husband (who was also David's friend). In pouring out his heart, David pleaded with God, saying "against you, and you alone, have I sinned" (verse 4). David knew that the sorrow he brought on Bathsheba, the betrayal and violence against Uriah, and the resulting pain that came to him and his family were nothing compared to the breach in relationship he experienced with God. Sin is sin because it brings relational harm. Every breach in relationship, every attack against love is caused by sin. And every act of disobedience against God's rule is inherently an attack against God, because he intends his design, which is for perfect love, to prevent us from hurting each other.

When we react in anger, when we choose to withdraw our love from another, when we choose to satisfy our own desires at the expense of someone else, we are not only sinning against that person, we are rebelling against God's design, which is *for perfect love*. His design isn't about enslaving us. It's about providing us

FORGIVENESS HAS BEGUN . . .

* when you see the ones who have hurt you with spiritual eyes;

* when, rather than wishing them harm, you desire that the ones who have offended you will get the opportunity to reconcile themselves to God;

* when you learn to apologize for your own wrongs;

* when you experience the gratitude that comes from grace;

* when you keep short accounts, crucifying your own pride and desire to be right, and choosing the power of love over the power of vengeance.

freedom to love others without harm. Yet we all fail at it. We all have, we all do, we all will.

Sometimes the hardest person to forgive is yourself. There is nothing like the feeling of letting yourself down, of walking through temptation, sin, and consequence from beginning to end. And when you get to that place, even when you've pleaded with God, even when you've confessed your sin to others, you can still feel stuck in the mud of your mistake.

Stories like David's give us all hope. If you've ever thought you were too bad for God to forgive, if you've ever felt beyond his loving grasp, if you've thought your story is too much for him, let me assure you, there is a person in Scripture for you. I am overwhelmed that God, in his goodness, chooses to count among the

Sometimes the hardest person to forgive is yourself.

heroes and heroines of faith many broken, wounded, and wound-inflicting people. These are the people he uses to bring his message of forgiveness, power, and love to our world. In Psalm 51:8, David asks for *God* to give him back his joy again. In verse 12, David asks of *God*, "Restore to me again the joy of your salvation, and make me willing to obey you." We find a message of hope amidst David's despair. And that hope is not from David's effort but from his contrite spirit that asks *God* to do what he cannot do for himself.

This is the she's-got-issues mantra: we've all got issues. You and I can't solve them, but *God can*. Forgiving yourself is not a five-step process you can just make happen. Forgiving yourself is what God does in you when you ask him to restore your joy. You will stay stuck in the mud of unforgiveness when you try to do it yourself. You will be left with the pain of your sin for a lifetime if you don't open yourself to the receiving of God's grace.

David finishes the psalm by offering God one thing in response for his grace: to pass it on. He promises that he will use his own sin as a way to teach sinners so that they might repent. David doesn't just ask for a private and personal reception of grace, but offers to use the ugliest of his sin to bring God glory. Wow. That takes guts, but what an incredible exchange! God will take your ugly, cover you with his joy, and send you out to bring other sinners to himself with your own story. But sometimes your story involves another level of forgiveness: forgiving God.

FORGIVING GOD

There is nothing like deliberate wrongdoing to make you question everything. When you experience evil, you have to reconcile all kinds of beliefs about the world. Perhaps the ideas of hell, evil, judgment, and demons are unsettling to you. Perhaps you've been taught to believe that all people are inherently good; that the only reason people are deliberately cruel is because of their own pain; that somehow you can escape unscathed if you just stay in church, do what the Bible says, and hang around only "nice" people.

But the events of our day, from 9/11 to the wars raging around the globe to the global sex trade, should shake us out of this warm, fuzzy theology about humanity. From existential concerns about why bad things happen to good people to closer-to-home issues like "Why is my life not going the way I planned?" we can harbor deep resentment and anger. We aren't sure who to blame, but somebody must be at fault for the mess in our lives! Sometimes we turn the pain onto ourselves, shouldering the blame of the world and staggering under its weight. We are left in a state of paralyzed helplessness, beaten by our resentment and the shame of believing we are the creators of all the bad in our lives.

Conversely, we may push that blame out. We blame everyone and everything for the ways life has let us down. We are not very enjoyable people to be with, as our blame storm hangs over us. We have fury in our hands and in our eyes, and in our wrath we are constantly looking for an object to fire upon.

Whether we blame ourselves or blame others, in the end, we are miserable. We seek happiness but cannot find it. Peace is nowhere to be found, and nothing brings us joy. We are the living dead. We may believe in God, but we don't believe him. Our faith is nothing more than talk, a box to be checked in our life checklist. But our God is bigger than our hurt, and we have an option when we're in this place.

My friend Ann-Douglas is a living example of a woman who has wrestled with God and come out better for it. We talked over a glass of lemonade, and I was transfixed by the passion in her eyes when she said, "I know God wanted me to wrestle with him. I really felt like he told me we were about to 'take it to the mat.'" So here are her own words about what it means to forgive God:

As a child, I always dreamed about what my adult life would be like. Now, at thirty, my current reality has yet to meet those dreams and expectations for several reasons, but mainly because I'm still single. I spent years wondering what God was doing and becoming more and more angry when relationships would turn sour. Why wasn't God answering my prayers for a partner? Was I holding on to this desire too strongly? Was there some sin in my heart that I had to be completely free of before God would give me this gift?

In my early twenties I experienced a spiritual lethargy and emotional depression that continued on and off for several years. During this time, I came across the Gerard Manley Hopkins poem: "Thou art indeed just, Lord, if I contend with thee; but, sir, so what I plead is just."[5]

I was a little frightened when I realized that I shared his complaint. I appreciated how he approached God with complete respect; however, it struck an uncomfortable chord in me when I fully understood what he was saying to God: that his plea, his complaint, is also just and therefore valid. Though fearful, I found myself identifying with the poet's grievance and began to understand that the emotional turmoil I had been experiencing was rooted in anger toward God. My prayers began to paraphrase Hopkins's words: "I know you are the Almighty and that you are completely just in what you ordain, but my plea is just as well! I've been obedient to you and yet you still withhold this blessing I long for."

It was a daunting thing for me to come before God and admit that I had a just complaint against him. After all, he created the universe, he has righteous anger, he is the most powerful being our finite minds can imagine. It is important for me to be aware of this when I approach him in prayer, because it is the truth. But I also must keep in mind that he is a God of compassion and he chose to redeem us through Christ. God is fully aware of the anger and complaints that I have against him and he is strong enough to accept them! He longs for me to be honest with not only him, but also myself. I've realized that he welcomes our complaints when we come with an attitude of awe, respect, and total honesty. And when honesty is there, forgiveness can begin to take place.

The book of Habakkuk is surprisingly comforting to me. The book is about Habakkuk's complaints to God. He does not withhold his anger toward God even to the point of questioning God's tolerance for injustice and destruction. God's answer is not a favorable one; Habakkuk's response to the answer is important:

> Though the fig tree does not bud
>   and there are no grapes on the vines,
> though the olive crop fails
>   and the fields produce no food . . .
> yet I will rejoice in the LORD,
>   I will be joyful in God my Savior. (Habakkuk 3:17-18, NIV)

Now I am able to acknowledge my frustration toward God and offer up those prayers of disappointment. I allow him to bring me to a place of forgiveness, and I begin to praise him regardless of my pain. I have found that when I praise God even in the midst of my hurt and anger, an odd thing begins to happen; the peace that passes all understanding finds its way in.

The books written on the process of forgiveness could fill a library, and we have only a few pages. If this chapter or book has opened your eyes to some deeper issues, let me first tell you that healing is closer at hand once you recognize your need for it. It takes strength to recognize your need for help. *Bold Love* by Dan Allender and Tremper Longman (see Further Resources) may provide further direction. If this thorny weed is too strongly rooted for you to pull up by yourself, invite someone into the process. Talking with a Christian counselor, a pastor, or a wise friend may provide the extra support you need to extract this root and free up space in your heart for love and freedom to thrive.

SPACE BAR

A PRAYER

Dear God, if there's ever an issue where I understand my need for you, it's in this one. Sometimes I just can't muster the strength I need to forgive. God, I open myself up to you. Please show me if there is any unforgiveness in me—for you, for others, or for myself—and enable me to accept your grace and pass that on freely. God, please increase my compassion for others and give me courage to forgive and to share my own story in a way that helps people turn to you. Amen.

A JOURNALING EXERCISE

Does your testimony involve forgiveness? Take a few minutes to think, write, and pray about how God has grown you through the process of forgiving yourself, someone else, or him. Consider sharing that story with someone else. If the idea of sharing makes you balk, journal about what makes you nervous or uneasy about opening up.

FOR GROUP DISCUSSION

1. Have you ever struggled with long-standing unforgiveness toward someone? Has it been resolved? If so, how?

2. If you have had a significant forgiveness experience, what helped you heal?

3. What do you do in order to "keep short accounts" with loved ones? How do you reconcile with those who've wounded you?

4. Do you need to grow in (a) letting go of grudges or (b) confronting unresolved conflict with a person who's wronged you? What is the next step you might take in that process?

Hear Nicole speak about the power of forgiveness. Snap the code with your smartphone or visit the link below.

www.tyndal.es/ShesGotIssues13

CHAPTER 14

LIVING THE LOVE (WITH ISSUES)

It's not having what you want,
It's wanting what you've got.
SHERYL CROW

WE'LL END THIS BOOK WHERE WE BEGAN: on my front porch. That's the place where I started to wonder if being a Christian was supposed to truly transform my life—not just give me some rules to live by but create a life bursting with love. To see others, not for their annoyances or criticisms or weaknesses, but as individuals fiercely loved by God. To respond to people, not through my own personality or filter, but by the directives of the Holy Spirit and my subsequent obedience. Would I ever be able to get past my tendencies to control, to compare, to act in anger?

In retrospect, I'm learning that perhaps the biggest problem was never my issues. My biggest problem was the lie I so desperately wanted to believe: that Jesus works *despite* my issues or *around* my issues. But now I believe the truth: he wants to work right *through* my issues. C. S. Lewis says that "what one calls the interruptions are precisely one's real life—the life God is sending one day by day: what one calls one's 'real life' is a phantom of one's own imagination."[1] My issues—your issues—are not mere interruptions in the quest to get on with real life.

The process of working through these issues is what theologians term *sanctification*. Sanctification, or refinement or character building or testing, or whatever you want to call it, is the lifelong process of being transformed into the likeness of Jesus. It begins when we surrender our lives to him and will continue until we stand before him in heaven. This part of Christianity is about a living, thriving relationship with God. This is the place where we experience the deep intimacy with Jesus during our life on earth.

Because I love when things are finished, I've always wanted to rush this process. Along with millions of other Americans, I've wanted the quick fix. I've wanted the solution; I've wanted Jesus to write lists and steps and action plans for making my life work. What I haven't wanted, what I've kicked and screamed against, is the reality of my own issues. These are the persistent places and patterns that stick around and suck peace out of my soul like a powerful vacuum cleaner. I've just wanted them fixed and finished—and fast.

But sanctification is about the very interruptions and issues I want to ignore. It's in these places that I have the opportunity to experience the deficit of my own heart and the amazing filling, the over-the-top abundance of life lived to the glory of God. Rather than being a woman without issues, I've learned that I'm a woman with issues who gets to boast about living in an active, present, powerful relationship with the God of the universe.

And this is what he offers you, too. Will he change you? Absolutely. Will you be perfect? Not on this earth! Jesus is the way and the truth and the life. The rich life he promises does not come through the things we possess, the successes we rack up, or the affirmation we receive. Yet it is a hearty and abundant life after all.

THE HEALTHY WOMAN: HEARTY AND ABUNDANT

Hearty and abundant? Those words don't seem to sum up what I'm trying to become. They sound like the description for a can of soup. I don't want to be soup. I want to be beautiful and elegant and smart and witty. But hearty and abundant might be much closer descriptors of what Jesus offers us. *Hearty* is defined as warm-hearted and affectionate; genuine and sincere; completely devoted; exuberant.[2] Hearty is about a full-of-life heart.

In Ezekiel 11:19 God speaks to his cherished Israelites and to all who would come to know him through Jesus, saying, "I will . . . put a new spirit within them. I will take away their hearts of stone and give them tender hearts instead." We can be women with new, unrestrained, hearty hearts!

When Jesus met a she's-got-issues woman at a well, he promised her this kind of new-heart experience, saying that the water he could give was from a whole new spring. That source has an endless supply and will last forever (see John 4:14).

When we invite Christ into our lives, he gives us the Holy Spirit to dwell within us and open up that spring of life to us. When the Spirit sets up shop, he begins the renovation work in our hearts. He hammers out the stony places so that our hearts can flow freely with Christ's living water. The best work of the Spirit is done in pounding through our issues so that we can invite God in to do his work.

Living the love happens when we have a new source of strength and peace in the center of our being. Not only does this new heart help us love those around us better, it compels us to love in bigger and greater ways. The Spirit who dwells within us begins to direct us to places where we can exercise our new heart. He compels us to lay down everything in our lives for the sake of his great gift. We experience our own miracle when our hearts change, and our response is lifelong devotion to obey his way.

If you've experienced this refinement, you are forever changed. That's because the process of sanctification always brings abundance to our lives. So what attributes bring this kind of abundance?

Refinement brings abundance

Psalm 66:10 says that God will test us and will refine us like silver. And in doing so, he will bring us to a place of abundance. Earlier this week I talked with a friend about the ups and downs of life. Because of her uncertain future and a lack of direction, she is questioning everything about some recent decisions. But after quieting her heart and spending some time journaling, her new heart was beating fast. "God has brought me through so much pain in my life. He has always been faithful. He can handle it. I could trust him then and I can trust him now," she said.

> The process of sanctification always brings abundance to our lives.

This is not the quote of a woman who has no issues. These words didn't come easily and they didn't come without doubt and confusion. But the words did come, evidence that her trust in the Lord is growing. That's abundance.

Honesty brings abundance

We do not receive God's blessings when we live in deceit. The world deceives us, offering claims and promises that it can never deliver. People deceive us, serving as emotional substitutes and becoming the objects of our worship. And we deceive ourselves, buying into all kinds of beliefs and lies about what will make us truly happy. This is not something we deal with once and then never struggle with again. This is the reality of living in a world in which we are strangers.

The Bible says that at one time, we were strangers and foreigners to God (see Ephesians 2:12-13). But once we accept Jesus as our Savior, we are adopted into his family even though we remain in the world that we have turned away from. We go from being strangers to God to strangers in this world (see 1 Peter 2:11).

I spent one summer living in Australia when I was in college. For six weeks, I was immersed in Australian culture. At first glance, it didn't seem much different from America. The people spoke English, ate chicken, and filled up their cars with gas. But then I began to see the ways in which it wasn't quite the same. They used several terms and phrases we don't use here. They ate only free-range chicken, and gas was sold by the (very expensive) liter. By the end of the six weeks, I had developed a lifelong love of Nutella and the phrase "no worries." It took only six weeks for me to adapt and adopt some of their ways as my own.

As an American Christian woman, I don't look all that different from typical American women. We dress alike and use similar terms. I shop in the same stores and send my kids to the same schools. And without vigilance, I will adapt more and more to the way of the majority rather than God's way.

This is not a call to homeschool our kids or ditch all our non-Christian friends. Rather, this is our opportunity to open our eyes to the reality of our world. We must be honest—gut-level, searingly honest—about the ways we are influenced by the world around us, with our issues old and new, and with our need for God in the moment-to-moment details of our lives. We need Christian sisters who hold us, not to the standard of our neighbors or culture, but to the standard of obedience to a life transformed by Christ.

It is in this honesty that we experience abundance. God promises that he will release abundance from his own house and that he's looking to give his love to those with "honest hearts" (Psalm 36:10). We are given new hearts. We are given honest hearts. Our hearts are guided in truth because the Holy Spirit, the "Spirit of truth" (John 16:13), dwells within them. Our issues need no longer blind and deceive us. The freedom of honesty? That's abundance.

Faithfulness brings abundance

Our small church staff doubles in size in the summer, when we employ interns to work in our student ministry. Recently as we said good-bye to our most recent group of interns, we spent some time sharing encouraging words about the work they had done. As I looked around the table at each of them, the word that came to mind was *faithfulness*.

These young men and women had devoted their summer to being faithful. They showed up and loved students even when they didn't have much to give. They kept serving even when serving got mundane and the work grew boring. They worshiped, prayed, and sought God even when their own emotions and doubts swirled around them like a funnel cloud.

I believe that God will bless that faithfulness with abundance in their lives. That abundance isn't about driving an SUV with navigation. It's an abundance of opportunities to see God work. This summer, I experienced these interns experiencing God. Jesus said, "To those who use well what they are given, even more will be given, and they will have an abundance" (Matthew 25:29). I watched my friend Cody watch middle schoolers worship with tears in his eyes. I watched my friend Stacie share her life in a way that helped high school girls be honest with themselves. I watched my friend Kristy glow with God's gifting as she testified to reasons why we praise God—not from her own place of abundance but from God's abundance.

Being with them made me want to be faithful. I want to be a

person who says what she means. I want to be a person who stays the course even when the road gets dark. I want to be a person who believes in the promises of God even when it seems foolish to keep hoping. This is what faithfulness means to me. The fruit of faithfulness? That's abundance.

Listening to the Holy Spirit brings abundance

Most of the practical helps in this book have really pointed you to only one thing: the need to listen to the Holy Spirit within you. After I once taught a Bible study, a friend told me she overheard another woman say, "I don't get excited and understand Scripture like Nicole does. I wish I had a Bible and Nicole on my nightstand." Now, while I admit the irony that you kind of have me on your nightstand now, you have something much better when you invite Christ to reign in your heart: you have the Holy Spirit.

The Holy Spirit is called our Counselor, Encourager, Truth-Teller. The Holy Spirit is like your divine conscience, speaking into your soul to keep you from sin and to lead you to minister to others with the love of Jesus. Not only does the Holy Spirit direct you in this ministry, he also ministers to you. Romans 8:26 says, "The Holy Spirit helps us in our distress. For we don't even know what we should pray for, nor how we should pray. But the Holy Spirit prays for us with groanings that cannot be expressed in words." There have been many issue-laden moments when the only thing my heart could muster up was the feeling that I needed to pray. I didn't know what to pray or how to pray or even what I wanted out of prayer. What a promise it is that the indwelt presence of God lifts me up and prays on behalf of me!

The passage goes on to declare that "the Spirit pleads for us believers in harmony with God's own will" (Romans 8:27). Right now, in this moment, the Spirit is talking to God about you. The Spirit is interceding on your behalf, on my behalf, so that the will of God is done. If you've ever been woken in the middle of the night with someone on your heart, you've experienced this. The Spirit within you is summoning you to be part of God's work. This is no small thing! This is the God of the universe moving and working and inviting you into the mysterious corporation of his saints joining with his Spirit to carry out his will.

When you begin the practice of listening to the Holy Spirit by working through your own issues, you will get much more than healing and peace for yourself. You will get the status of VIP in God's Kingdom. That's abundance!

Feeding our soul brings abundance

We know we must have food for our bodies to live. We can go for a long time without food, but when we do, we grow weak, unfocused, and confused. We cannot just stuff ourselves at one meal and expect to be nourished for the next month, either. Our bodies function best when they receive healthy food at regular intervals.

Our souls aren't much different. We cannot front-load our spiritual life at a retreat or through a book or one church service and expect to be nourished forever. We cannot go without spiritual food for a long time and expect our souls to be hearty and abundant.

As children, food literally grows us. As adults, food, if used correctly, nourishes us so we can thrive and work and sustain our mature bodies. Likewise, at times the food of God's Word actually grows us into new, mature beings. At other times that same food sustains us and keeps us thriving in our work. The end result may be different, but the means stay the same. There will never be a time when we "arrive" as bodies that don't need food. There will never be a time when we "arrive" as Christians and no longer need nourishment. That is why I love God's invitation to us:

Come, all you who are thirsty, come to the waters; and you who have no money, come, buy and eat! . . . Listen, listen to me, and eat what is good, and your soul will delight in the richest of fare. Give ear and come to me; hear me, that your soul may live. (Isaiah 55:1-3, NIV)

There have been times of great stress and burden when I was deeply peaceful with the Lord. There have been times of worldly abundance when I was a mess. We must not allow ourselves to be deceived into thinking that our circumstances determine the state of our souls. One of God's great promises is that his love and peace reach far beyond our earthly experience. If this were not true, how could we stand it? How could we ever imagine Jesus' love reaching into the slums and street corners of our nation, or into the darkest corners of a brothel in Eastern Europe?

David said in Psalm 51:10, "Create in me a clean heart, O God. Renew a right spirit within me." Our new, honest, clean hearts are in need of renewal. I think all of us know deep down when our spirit is *right*. We know when we have peace that keeps a quiet center in our souls. We *Don't be deceived into thinking that your circumstances determine the state of your soul.* know when we have a deeper joy that reaches beyond any pain. And this right spirit, if we are to pay attention, does not depend on our circumstances.

Because a clean heart, a right spirit, and a transformed mind are available to us, because Jesus says, "Yes, following me is supposed to actually change you," we must pay attention to how we feed our souls. Yesterday a coworker of mine said, "I think we make the soul much too nebulous. What if we imagined it as a much 'weightier' part of us that requires its own care, much like we care for our bodies?"

So what does this soul care look like? It looks like many of the suggestions in this book. It looks like regular meals of worship music, Scripture, spiritual reading, and time with friends who sharpen and encourage you in your faith. It looks like participation with a community of believers. It looks like love, for your family, for your coworkers, for your neighbors. It looks like that middle-of-the-night wake-up call when you find yourself praying deeply, even groaning for another's heart and life. It looks like tears of godly sorrow when you know you've done wrong. It looks like tears of joy as you accept your status as beloved even in your mess. This, my friends, is abundant life.

THE END OF THE BEGINNING

This is the end of this book, but not a real ending, because my prayer for you is that this is the beginning. My prayer for you is that you have experienced a holy moment somewhere along this path, a place where you turned from an old way and realized that you would never be the same.

Because the mantra of the she's-got-issues soul is that you and I aren't perfect, but we can choose growth. We choose growth when it hurts; we choose growth when it drives us to lie on our faces before God. We choose growth when we are challenged and succeed, and we choose growth when we fail. We choose growth because it's built into the fiber of our souls to be reborn into Christ, to keep in step with his Spirit within us, and to "let God transform [us] by changing the way [we] think" (Romans 12:2). It's not the easy path. But it's the dynamic, holy, and beautiful one.

> THE *SHE'S GOT ISSUES* CREED
> *When I'm controlling, I'll choose to surrender to God's way.*
> *When I'm insecure, I'll seek the truth.*

When I'm stuck comparing, I'll look for new perspective.
When I'm scared, I'll trust God to bring peace.
When I'm angry, I'll invite God to handle me.
When I'm hurt, I'll forgive.
I won't be perfect—but I will be honest.
I won't always do it right—but I will apologize.
I won't always be settled—but I will always keep seeking.

SPACE BAR

A PRAYER

This is growth: to write your own prayer here. I invite you to take The *She's Got Issues* Creed and make it personal. What is your prayer as you finish this study?

_____

_____

_____

A JOURNALING EXERCISE

Label the top of your page "I'm learning . . ." and then give yourself ten to fifteen minutes to flip through the book or your Bible and pick up what's resonated with you. Write phrases or sentences to complete the "I'm learning" prompt. This will serve as a remembrance of this season in your life and what God is showing you. That is a valuable record to keep and recall.

_____

_____

_____

_____

FOR GROUP DISCUSSION

1. How do you feel about being hearty and abundant? Does your life reflect the state of your heart? Why or why not?

2. Which of the "abundance" tenets do you most resonate with? Explain.

    needing refinement

    choosing honesty

    staying faithful

    listening to the Spirit

    feeding your soul

3. If the major goal of your spiritual life is growth, where have you grown through this book? Which issue have you seen the most change in?

4. What would you add to The She's Got Issues Creed for yourself? What's one thing you want to share with someone as you close this book?

Listen to a special message from Nicole to you, as you finish reading *She's Got Issues*. Snap the code with your smartphone or visit the link below.

www.tyndal.es/ShesGotIssues14

Further Resources

TO FIND A COUNSELOR
American Association of Christian Counselors resources include a national referral
   network of Christian counselors at www.aacc.net.
Focus on the Family offers a counselor search engine at www.FocusOnTheFamily.com.

FOR FURTHER READING
Allender, Dan B., and Tremper Longman III. *Bold Love*. Colorado Springs: NavPress,
   1992.
Allender, Dan B. *To Be Told: God Invites You to Coauthor Your Future*. Colorado
   Springs: WaterBrook, 2005.
Chole, Alicia Britt. *Anonymous: Jesus' Hidden Years . . . and Yours*. Nashville: Thomas
   Nelson, 2006.
Eldredge, John. *Waking the Dead: The Glory of a Heart Fully Alive*. Nashville: Thomas
   Nelson, 2006.
Foster, Richard. *Celebration of Discipline: The Path to Spiritual Growth*. New York:
   HarperCollins, 1998.
Hurnard, Hannah. *Hinds' Feet on High Places*. Carol Stream, IL: Tyndale, 1975.
Kreeft, Peter. *Back to Virtue: Traditional Moral Wisdom for Modern Moral Confusion*.
   San Francisco: Ignatius Press, 1992.
Manning, Brennan. *The Importance of Being Foolish: How to Think Like Jesus*. New
   York: HarperCollins, 2005.
Manning, Brennan. *Ruthless Trust: The Ragamuffin's Path to God*. New York:
   HarperCollins, 2002.
Miller, Paul. *Love Walked Among Us: Learning to Love like Jesus*. Colorado Springs:
   NavPress, 2001.
Moore, Beth. *Breaking Free: Discover the Victory of Total Surrender*. Nashville: B&H
   Publishers, 2007.
Moore, Beth. *Living Free: Learning to Pray God's Word* (Bible study). Nashville:
   Lifeway Christian Resources, 2002.
Nouwen, Henri J. M. *Out of Solitude: Three Meditations on the Christian Life*. Notre
   Dame, IN: Ave Maria Press, 2004.

Notes

CHAPTER 1: CHEAP PLASTIC SOULS

1. Brennan Manning, *The Importance of Being Foolish: How to Think Like Jesus* (New York: HarperCollins, 2005), 49.
2. A small sample of such passages includes Exodus 34:6; 2 Chronicles 30:9; Nehemiah 9:17; and Psalm 145:8.

CHAPTER 2: MORE THAN MEDIOCRE (A.K.A. THE GREEN SQUARE)

1. Inga Kiderra, "Spoiler Alert: Stories Are Not Spoiled by 'Spoilers,'" UC San Diego News Center, August 10, 2011. http://ucsdnews.ucsd.edu/newsrel/soc /2011_08spoilers.asp.
2. See 1 Samuel 18 through 2 Samuel 12.
3. "This is the one I esteem: he who is humble and contrite in spirit, and trembles at my word." (Isaiah 66:2, NIV)
4. See Psalms 18:27; 25:9; 147:6; and Proverbs 3:34 for a sample of what God says about the humble.
5. "Blessing," *Wikipedia*, http://en.wikipedia.org/wiki/Blessing.
6. Hannah Hurnard, *Hinds' Feet on High Places* (Carol Stream, IL: Tyndale House Publishers, 1975), 179.

CHAPTER 3: I'M NOT CONTROLLING (I JUST LIKE MY LATTE EXTRA HOT)

1. Elisabeth Kübler-Ross, *Death: The Final Stage of Growth* (New York: Touchstone, 1986), 93.
2. See Isaiah 61:3; 2 Corinthians 12:9; and Romans 8:28.
3. For a brief overview of the Keirsey Temperament Sorter, go to http://www.keirsey .com/sorter/instruments2.aspx?partid=0.
4. "Locus of Control," *Wikipedia*, http://en.wikipedia.org/wiki/locus_of_control.
5. Salvatore R. Maddi, *Personality Theories: A Comparative Analysis* (Prospect Heights, IL: Waveland Press, 1996).
6. Judith Viorst, *Imperfect Control: Our Lifelong Struggles with Power and Surrender* (New York: Fireside Press, 1999), 265.

CHAPTER 4: SURRENDERING THE KUNG-FU CONTROL GRIP

1. Commentators generally agree that the "us" of Genesis 1:26 refers to the Trinity. See also John 1:1 ("In the beginning was the Word . . . and the Word was God") as well as the Nicene Creed: "We believe in the Holy Spirit, the Lord and giver of Life."
2. See Ephesians 4:15.
3. See 1 Peter 4:8.
4. See commentary on Genesis 50:15-21 in Matthew Henry, *Commentary on the Whole Bible*, ed. Leslie F. Church (Grand Rapids, MI: Zondervan, 1961), 70. http://www.biblestudytools.com/commentaries/matthew-henry-complete/genesis/50.html?p=3.
5. Corrie Cutrer, "The Goodness of God: Why Author Nancy Guthrie Believes Submission Is Really about Trust," *Kyria*, March/April 2011, http://christianitytoday.imirus.com/Mpowered/book/vkyria11/i3/p8.
6. Isaiah 30:21.
7. L. B. Cowman, *Streams in the Desert* (Grand Rapids, MI: Zondervan, 1997), 229.

CHAPTER 5: INSIDIOUS INSECURITY

1. Some statements adapted from http://www.blogthings.com/areyouaninsecuregirlquiz and http://opentheword.org/index.php?option=com_content&view=article&id=156:how-insecure-are-you&catid=72:worry&Itemid=193.
2. See http://rachelheldevans.com/insecurity. Rachel is also the author of *Evolving in Monkey Town* (Grand Rapids, MI: Zondervan, 2010).
3. Randall Parker, "Babies Prefer to Stare at Beautiful Faces," *FuturePundit*, September 7, 2004, http://www.futurepundit.com/archives/002338.html.
4. For a fascinating review of appearance research, see Kate Fox, "Mirror, Mirror: A Summary of Research Findings on Body Image," Social Issues Research Centre, 1997, http://www.sirc.org/publik/mirror.html.
5. Pauline Rose Clance and Suzanne Imes, "The Imposter Phenomenon in High Achieving Women: Dynamics and Therapeutic Intervention," *Psychotherapy Theory, Research and Practice* 15, no. 3 (Fall 1978). http://www.paulineroseclance.com/pdf/ip_high_achieving_women.pdf.

CHAPTER 6: ATTACHING YOUR ANCHOR

1. *Hebrew-Greek Key Word Study Bible, New International Version*, ed. Spiros Zodhiates (Chattanooga, TN: AMG Publishers, 1996), 1651.
2. Francis Chan, "Living in Light of Eternity" (sermon, Cornerstone Church, Simi Valley, CA, March 8, 2009), http://www.youtube.com/watch?v=86dsfBbZfWs.
3. Ajith Fernando, "Being a Christian: What Difference Does it Make?" in *This We Believe: The Good News of Jesus Christ for the World*, edited by John N. Akers, John H. Armstrong, and John D. Woodbridge (Grand Rapids, MI: Zondervan, 2000), 125.
4. Mike Crawford, "Words to Build a Life On," copyright © 2004, BMI.

CHAPTER 7: THE COMPARISON GAME

1. Margaret Delores Isom, "The Social Learning Theory." November 30, 1988, http://criminology.fsu.edu/crimtheory/bandura.htm.

2. William Young, *The Shack* (Newbury Park, CA: Windblown Media, 2007), 126. I've borrowed Young's parade description that was originally a metaphor to describe pain and death, but I think it works equally well to describe the lie of comparisons with others' lives.

3. Anthony de Mello, *The Way to Love* (New York: Image Books, 1995), 125.

4. William C. Crain, *Theories of Development* (Upper Saddle River, NJ: Prentice-Hall, 1985), 118–136.

5. *Easton's 1897 Bible Dictionary,* s.v. "justice," accessed June 1, 2010, http://dictionary.reference.com/browse/justice.

CHAPTER 8: QUITTING THE COMPARISON GAME

1. Hugh MacLeod, *Ignore Everybody and 39 Other Keys to Creativity* (New York: Portfolio Group, 2009).

2. Philip Edgcumbe Hughes, *The New International Commentary on the New Testament: The Second Epistle to the Corinthians* (Grand Rapids, MI: Eerdmans Publishing, 1962), 367.

CHAPTER 9: KNOW FEAR; NO FEAR?

1. See "Facts and Statistics," Anxiety Disorders Association of America, http://www.adaa.org/about-adaa/press-room/facts-statistics.

2. Some of these statements are adapted from resources found in "Generalized Anxiety Disorder Assessment Tool," http://www.harthosp.org/InstituteOfLiving/AnxietyDisordersCenter/GeneralizedAnxietyDisorder/OnlineAssessment/default.aspx.

3. Paul Tillich, *The Eternal Now* (New York: Charles Scribner's Sons, 1963), chapter 1.

CHAPTER 10: THE BIG LEAP FROM FEAR TO FREEDOM

1. Neil Anderson and Rich Miller, *Freedom from Fear: Overcoming Worry and Anxiety* (Eugene, OR: Harvest House, 1999), 20.

2. Katie Couric, ed., *The Best Advice I Ever Got: Lessons from Extraordinary Lives* (New York: Random House, 2011). Stockett's essay was reprinted at http://www.more.com/kathryn-stockett-help-best-seller.

3. Old Testament lexical aid for *sar'appiym* found in Spiros Zodhiates, ed., *Hebrew-Greek Key Word Study Bible, New International Version* (Chattanooga, TN: AMG Publishers, 1996).

4. Wil Hernandez, *Henri Nouwen: A Spirituality of Imperfection* (Mahwah, NJ: Paulist Press, 2006), 31.

5. Shawn McDonald, "All I Need," Birdwing Music © 2004.

CHAPTER 11: ANGER IS FOR FOOLS LIKE ME

1. Laurie Davies, "25 Years of Saving Lives," Mothers Against Drunk Driving, http://www.madd.org/about-us/history/madd25thhistory.pdf.
2. Some statements are loosely based on the assessment at CompassionPower.com, http://compassionpower.com/Anger/.
3. R. P. Walters, *Anger: Yours, Mine, and What to Do about It* (Grand Rapids, MI: Zondervan, 1981). This book looks old and out of date but is an incredibly helpful resource on anger!
4. Ibid.

CHAPTER 12: HOW TO CHANGE A WICKED WITCH

1. Jerry Bridges, *Respectable Sins: Confronting the Sins We Tolerate* (Colorado Springs: NavPress, 2007), 122.
2. Julie Ann Barnhill, *She's Gonna Blow: Real Help for Moms Dealing with Anger* (Eugene, OR: Harvest House, 2001).
3. Keri Wyatt Kent, *Rest: Living in Sabbath Simplicity* (Grand Rapids, MI: Zondervan, 2009).
4. Attributed to Ambrose Bierce, see http://www.quotegarden.com/anger.html.
5. Jen Hatmaker. "Fighters," (blog entry), July 6, 2011, http://jenhatmaker.com/blog/2011/07/06/fighters.

CHAPTER 13: UNFORGIVENESS: UPROOTING THE BITTER WEED

1. "Learning to Forgive May Improve Well-Being," Mayo Clinic, January 2, 2008, http://www.mayoclinic.org/news2008-mchi/4405.html.
2. Amos 2:6 says, "This is what the Lord says: 'For three sins of Israel, even for four, I will not turn back my wrath'" (NIV). Frederick Dale Bruner, *Matthew: A Commentary, Volume 2: The Churchbook, Matthew 13–28* (Grand Rapids, MI: Eerdmans, 2007), 236.
3. Lewis Smedes, *Forgive and Forget: Healing the Hurts We Don't Deserve* (New York: HarperCollins, 1996), x.
4. Ibid., 29.
5. Gerard Manley Hopkins, "Thou Art Indeed Just, Lord, If I Contend," *Poems of Gerard Manley Hopkins*, ed. Robert Bridges (Whitefish, MT: Kessinger Publishing, 2004), 63.

CHAPTER 14: LIVING THE LOVE (WITH ISSUES)

1. C. S. Lewis, *Yours, Jack: Spiritual Direction from C. S. Lewis* (New York: HarperOne, 2008), 98.
2. Dictionary.com, s.v. "hearty," http://dictionary.reference.com/browse/hearty.

About the Author

NICOLE UNICE is a full-time mom and a part-time ministry leader and blogger. She is the contributing editor for Christianity Today's online community for women, *Gifted for Leadership*, and a regular columnist for *Kyria.com*. She is also a national speaker, known for bringing a fresh voice for a new generation and combining her love of storytelling with biblical insights. Nicole's first Bible study, *The Divine Pursuit: A Study of Jonah*, has been well received by groups around the country.

Nicole lives in Richmond, Virginia, and works and worships at Hope Church. She shares her life with an amazing husband, three awesome kids, and a whole community of teenagers and twentysomethings. Visit her website at www.nicoleunice.com to read her blog and find out about upcoming events.

A portion of the proceeds from this book will be donated to Midwives for Haiti, an organization devoted to helping reduce infant and maternal mortality in Haiti by educating Haitian women and providing prenatal care and skilled birth assistance. For more details, visit www.midwivesforhaiti.org.

Online Discussion Guide

TAKE YOUR TYNDALE READING
EXPERIENCE TO THE NEXT LEVEL

A FREE discussion guide for this book is available at
bookclubhub.net, perfect for sparking conversations in your
book group or for digging deeper into the text on your own.

www.bookclubhub.net

You'll also find free discussion guides for other Tyndale books,
e-newsletters, e-mail devotionals, virtual book tours, and more!

CP0070

Watch for the new
SHE'S GOT ISSUES
DVD curriculum experience,
coming in fall 2012!

CP0565

Sometimes you just can't sing out a hallelujah . . . but, well, maybe you could grumble one.

Have you been there? Sometimes life is just disappointingly different from what you dream. But what would happen if you turned to God—even during life's lowest moments—and managed to praise him, in whatever way you could? Is it possible you would be surprised at the many reasons you have to rejoice?

Grumble Hallelujah offers humor, candid stories, and solid scriptural backing that will help you see clearly just how your life is meant to be lived—and loved.

For Lisa Velthouse's whole life, Christianity had been about getting things right.

Yet after two decades of trying to earn God's okay, she found her faith was lonely, empty, and unsatisfying. Hungry for a deeper connection with God, Lisa gave up her favorite foods—sweets—hoping to somehow discover true sweetness and meaning in her faith. Until, one night at a wedding, Lisa denied herself the cake but failed in such a different, unexpected, and world-rocking way that it challenged everything she thought she knew about God and herself.

Craving Grace is the compelling true story of a faith dramatically changed: how in one woman's life God used a bitter heart, a broken promise, and the sweetness of honey to reveal the stunning wonder that is grace.

978-1-4143-3577-3

CP0478

How to get past whatever's holding you back—and start living a whole new story

An honest look at the holes in your life—and how to let God fill them

{w}hole

LISA WHITTLE

Foreword by George Barna

We all have holes in our lives—those things we lament about ourselves and that keep us from living the life God wants for us. But what if you discovered that the holes in your life are really the things that will ultimately make you . . . well, whole?

In *Whole*, Lisa Whittle shares the holes that rocked her world—and faith—to the core, and she challenges you to take an honest look at the holes in your own life. You'll gain a new understanding of who you really are—and what you were born to be and do—as you learn how God can fill any hole with his presence.

CP0551